Get your RSS into gear
Proven recommended and expert in rider claims

Rider Support Services

email rss@ridersupport.co.uk or telephone **020 8246 4900**

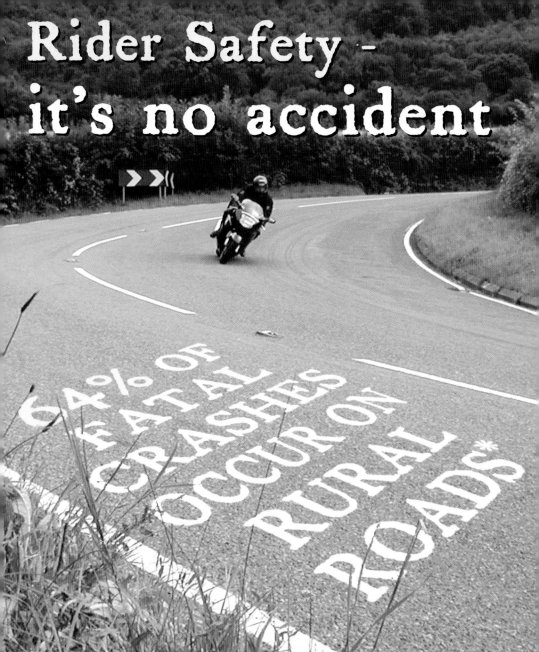

Rider Safety - it's no accident

64% OF FATAL CRASHES OCCUR ON RURAL ROADS*

* Source DfT

Gloucestershire
COUNTY COUNCIL

The South West Bike Guide

www.thePIEguide.com

Contents

www.thepieguide.com
Quality maps, Innovative delivery & Local content

Published by PIE Enterprises Ltd © 2007

PIE Enterprises Ltd and any of its sponsors take no responsibility whatsoever for any consequences of driving, parking or using any establishments in this guide. Every effort has been made to ensure the data on this map is as accurate as possible. Whilst the publishers would be grateful to learn of any errors, users should be aware that this information can change at any time. PIE Enterprises Ltd and our sponsors cannot accept any responsibility for loss thereby caused.

Information specific to this publication supplied by © PIE Enterprises Ltd 2007. All rights reserved. No reproduction by any method whatsoever of any part of this publication is permitted without prior written consent of the copyright owners.

General enquiries and trade sales
Telephone 0870 444 5434, Fax 0870 444 5437
Email: enquiries@thepieguide.com
Editor: Freddie Talberg

Information on fixed speed camera locations provided by Cyclops UK Ltd. © Copyright Cyclops™
www.cyclops-uk.com
POWERED BY Cyclops

☾ Collins

Specially produced for PIE Enterprises Ltd by Collins.

Mapping © Collins Bartholomew 2007

Supplementary information © PIE Enterprises Ltd 2007

ISBN: 978-0-9551711-5-4

Printed and bound in Croatia by Zrinski

Special thanks for help and support from:

PIE Enterprises Ltd:
Mike Hudson, Adnan Khan, Tomaz Vizintin, Lucy Robinson-Tillett, Peita Sims

PIE Advertising & Marketing:
Tony Young, Lucy Peel, Carolina Ana, David Francis

Our team of surveyors:
Mark King, Pawel Kamil Bloch

Local Content providers:
Jim Peel-Cross Chairman of BMF SouthWest Region and his dedicated helpers, Regional BMF members, Regional Riders Clubs and Associations & Regional Councils

Cover Design: Abdul Kadir

Cartographers: Collins Maps and Atlases

Introduction

Welcome to the BMF! We are the biggest and
most influential riders' rights organisation in
the UK and one of the largest in Europe.
Our aim is to promote, pursue and protect
the interests of all riders of motorcycles and
scooters in the UK.

Thanks for buying the PIE guide, which is a joint partnership to pilot getting great maps and local information to our members and riders, making them more visible by using quality maps put together by the PIE guide team. Your feedback on this and what else we can do in this guide would be greatly appreciated.

Apart from promoting the interests of all riders, whether riding for business or pleasure, there are other benefits to being a BMF member and this booklet indicates what's on offer. For example discounts are available to BMF members on a range of services including insurance, ferry bookings, breakdown cover, the National Motorcycle Museum, etc.

The BMF runs some great shows too; the BMF Show at Peterborough in May is the biggest outdoor motorcycle event of its type in Europe, but whether it's the big show or one of the smaller ones, in Kelso, in Kent or Tail End, again in Peterborough, they're fun – and as a member you get a substantial discount on admission! Our regional volunteers frequently organise local events and attend other shows – I hope you will be able to find something in your area, bringing bikers together.

You can also get involved yourself if you choose. If you'd like to, say, get involved in tackling your local authority on motorcycling issues but don't know where to start, we have a team of professionals and other volunteers who can help. We have many volunteers who marshal at the shows – you could join them. It's hard work but it's fun too. Or you might like to set up your own local bikers meet – let us know what you would like to do and we'll try to help. And finally, if you see any way we can improve the way we work, in whatever area, please get in touch to tell us.

And above all, get out there on your bike and enjoy! I hope to meet you some time!

Anna Zee, Chairwoman, BMF

MEMBER ENQUIRIES – 0116 284 53 90

"I saved £200 when I insured my Fireblade with Swinton"

Matt Cheek

Matt Cheek, 32, East Sussex.
Been riding for 1 year. 1 year no claims.
Loves the bends on the A272 near Petworth.

Rock bottom prices on motorbike insurance

Amazing rates for bikes over 500cc

Specialist schemes and bargain rates from top UK insurers

Excellent, friendly service from our expert bike team

0800 977 5067

Lines open: Monday to Friday 9am to 8pm, Saturday 9am to 5.30pm, Sunday 10am to 4pm

www.swintonbikes.co.uk

Swinton Bikes is a division of Swinton Group Limited, registered in England number 756681, is connected for the purposes of the Insurance Companies Regulations 1981 to MMA Insurance plc and Gateway Insurance Company Limited. Registered office: Swinton House, 6 Great Marlborough Street, Manchester M1 5SW. Calls may be recorded. Authorised and regulated by the Financial Services Authority.

TO ANYONE WHO EVER SAID "IT COULD NEVER BE DONE"

To register for exclusive updates on B-King visit www.suzukibking.co.uk
Final production model may vary from image shown.

Way of Life!

A CONCEPT BECOMES REALITY

The rider's website for maps and local information

www.roadsforbikes.com, parkingforbikes.com and roadsforbikes.com all go the extra mile to make sure riders have all the essential information you need when you're out and about in the UK, from route planning and speed camera locations to finding petrol stations and bike bays.

The site offers comprehensive in-depth mapping together with customised content for the bike community.

Features include:

☆ recommended roads

☆ car parks allowing bikes, highlighting those which are free and discounted

☆ bike bays

☆ bus lanes permitted for use by bikes

☆ locations of bike-friendly accommodation, bars, cafés and restaurants

☆ club meet sites

☆ motorcycle dealers, repair shops and training schools

☆ accident and emergency hospitals

New for this year is a routing facility, allowing you to create "your space". Registered users can plot routes, add notes, and upload photos to share with other riders. You will be able to up and download your routes to your GPS. Pre-register now at www.roadsforbikes.com

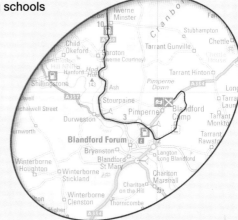

We'd love to hear what other features and functions you would like to see. Please send your comments by registering online or email today: feedback@roadsforbikes.com

Finally we have completed this long overdue guide. This guide was conceptualised some time ago and the BMF have been fantastic supporters of the concept and once we received the buy in and support from our sponsors Suzuki & RSS it was all go. So a special thanks to them.

PIE and the PIE guide are all about delivering a viable mapping product that is sustainable and fit for purpose mapping. We collate the appropriate blend of public (typically council) information, private data from businesses and augment with local rider related information. This information we verify and plot the locations on the mapping.

We have created a map of the whole South West region that is designed purely for riders. We have spent a lot of effort qualifying the recommended bike friendly sites of accommodation, cafés, bars and restaurants. What is interesting with our questionnaire for all sites, particularly bike friendly accommodation, is that businesses are appreciating more the importance of bike security, off road parking and drying rooms.

Highlighted roads/routes

It is my belief that we need to show some of the exciting roads in the region to enable you to link up your own routes/journeys for your trips and tours. At least with bike friendly sites on the map, you can plan these into your route.

We have included a selection of town plans in the region to help you find the location of parking bays, the rules on bus lane driving plus the location of car parks that provide free parking for bikes.

Top Tips

I have seen so many books advising on what to pack that we thought it would be better to hear from a local and experienced rider from the region and so ran a small competition between the training schools in the region to come up with their "top tips". I am pleased to say Martin Lambert from One to One Motorcycle Training based in Tuffley, Gloucester did a great job and shares his wisdom with us all.

I hope you enjoy this first in the Open Road Rider's Guide series, I personally would welcome feedback from you on your thoughts, how you use the guide, changes to the information shown and other features that would be of value to you. Our plan is to extend the range of regional guides based on the BMF regions to cover the UK. Adopting this concept we anticipate good local feedback and quality local insight. If you want to get involved creating our other regional guides I welcome your input.

Online version

We also run an online mapping service which now covers the UK and has parking information for the main UK cities and routes and bike friendly sites for the South West. So feel free to plot your own, store and share your own routes and upload or download these onto your GPS.

Thanks and enjoy.
Freddie
freddie@thePIEguide.com

Great Savings For All Members!

We value your membership of the BMF. It equips us to do our main job of campaigning – protecting, promoting and pursuing the interests of motorcyclists. At the same time, being a member of the BMF offers a number of benefits. Taking advantage of just one of these can save you more than the cost of a full year's membership of the BMF!

Breakdown Recovery

NCI Biker Rescue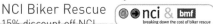

15% discount off NCI standard rates. Both UK and European cover available for any type or age of bike. NCI specialise in bike assistance and recovery but can also cover your car or you personally on any vehicle.

- NCI Comprehensive: Up to 1 hour roadside assistance. Recovery to home, original destination or garage. You pay £33.15
- Home Assist: Includes the details above plus assistance at home. You pay £63.75
- European: As the Comprehensive cover but extends to the specified European countries. You pay £72.00

Call NCI on 0800 783 6026 or click www.ncionline.co.uk

BMF Insurance
Bennetts

Bennetts the BMF's preferred insurance provider, offers BMF members exclusive discounts on insurance. Preferential rates have been negotiated to ensure that BMF members continue to receive value for money when it comes to bike insurance. BMF members can also benefit from further discounts on limited mileage, garaging and security. For fast and competitive quotes that give you instant cover call Bennetts on 0800 072 5943 or visit www.bennetts.co.uk. Bennetts is a trading name of BISL Limited. BISL Limited is authorised and regulated by the Financial Services Authority.

BMF Events

Entry discounts and exclusive camping at selected events throughout the year.

Hotel Savings
Intercontinental Hotel Group

Enjoy a 25% discount off weekend leisure breaks at over 300 Crowne Plaza, Holiday Inn & Express by Holiday Inn hotels throughout the UK, Ireland and Europe. To book from UK call 0870 400 8135 or visit www.ichotels.com/exclusive. To book from the Republic of Ireland please call 1-800 553155 Please quote 'Exclusive Rate.' For full terms & conditions visit www.ichotels.com/exclusive

Biker Legal Line

Open to all members, the Biker Legal Line offers access to firms of solicitors across the UK and Eire. Each firm is a BMF Corporate Member and offers advice from a qualified motorcycling solicitor. Individual Members have access to additional legal benefits. The number to call is 08000 856 243. The line is open from Monday – Thursday 9am-5pm, Friday 9am-4.30pm.

BMF Loans

Buying a new bike? Why not take advantage of a BMF Personal Loan available exclusively to BMF members. For a competitive quote, call free on 0800 517151 and quote BMF-AFFDISC. BMF – better biking for you, our members. Loans are available to UK Residents, aged 18 or over. MBNA Europe Bank Limited is authorised and regulated by the Financial Services Authority for the sale of general insurance. MBNA will monitor or record some phone calls. Registered Office Address: MBNA Europe Bank Limited, Stansfield House, Chester Business Park, Chester CH4 9QQ. Registered in England No. 2783251.

BMF Merchandise

BMF t-shirts, sweatshirts, polo shirts, caps and fleeces and much more supplied in high quality fabric and direct to your door. Also mugs, jigsaws, mousemats all personalised with your photo. There are so many items to choose from visit www.bmfshop.net to see what's on offer. BMF members get a 5% discount when they quote their membership number.

MEMBER ENQUIRIES - 0116 284 5390

Join the BMF

BMF members enjoy lots of great offers and discounts. If you or someone you know feel passionate about protecting your right to ride, fill in the form below. For renewals please call 0116 284 5390.

bmf
better biking

Join the BMF today and take advantage of all our great membership benefits!

I/We wish to join the BMF
and agree to abide by its rules

Your details:

Surname:.. Title: ....

First name(s):...
....

Date of Birth: .... Male: [ ] Female: [ ] (please tick)

Address: ....
....

Postcode:.......................... Daytime tel. no.:...............................

Email: ....

Joint member's details:

Surname: .... Title: ....

First name(s):...
....

Date of Birth: .... Male: [ ] Female: [ ] (please tick)

For membership renewals please telephone 0116 284 5390.

Membership prices: (please tick one box only)

Single membership: £26 [ ]   Fighting Fund donation: £...........

Joint membership: £32 [ ]   Total enclosed: £...........

Save on your membership by either: (please tick one box only)

Save £3 by paying by Direct Debit (please complete form overleaf) [ ]

Save £1 by enclosing your current affiliate (i.e. club) member card [ ]

Payment by debit / credit cards:

Please charge my: Mastercard [ ]   Visa [ ]   Switch [ ] (please tick)

Name on card: ....

Card no.:...

Security no.: (last 3 digits on reverse of card)...

Issue date: ....   Expiry date: ....

Issue no.: (Switch only) ....   Signature:....................................

Please make cheques payable to BMF.
Return completed forms to: BMF, Jack Wiley House,
25 Warren Park Way, Enderby, Leicestershire LE19 4SA.
Alternatively, telephone 0116 284 5390 with your card details.

LATEST NEWS AND INFO — BMF.CO.UK

This guarantee should be retained by the Payer.
THE DIRECT DEBIT GUARANTEE

- This Guarantee is offered by all Banks and Building Societies that take part in the Direct Debit Scheme.
- The efficiency and security of the Scheme is monitored and protected by your own Bank or Building Society.
- If the amounts to be paid or the payment dates change the British Motorcyclists Association will notify you 10 working days in advance of your account being debited or as otherwise agreed.
- If an error is made by the British Motorcyclists Association or your Bank or Building Society, you are guaranteed a full and immediate refund.
- You can cancel a Direct Debit at any time by writing to your Bank or Building Society.
- Please also send a copy of your letter to us.

Join the BMF and pay by Direct Debit to save £3 on our normal membership prices

Instruction to your Bank or Building Society to pay by Direct Debit

Please fill in the whole form and send to: BMF, Jack Wiley House, 25 Warren Park Way, Enderby, Leicester, LE19 4SA, UK

DIRECT Debit

Name and full postal address of your Bank or Building Society

To the Manager

Bank or Building Society

Address

Postcode

Name(s) of Account Holder(s)

Bank or Building Society account number

Branch sort code

Originator's identification number

9 4 1 6 4 0

Reference number (for BMF official use only)

Instructions to your Bank or Building Society
Please pay the British Motorcyclists Federation Direct Debits from the account detailed on this Instruction subject to the safeguards assured by the Direct Debit Guarantee. I understand that this instruction may remain with the British Motorcyclists Federation and, if so, will be passed on electronically to my Bank/Building Society.

Signature(s)

Date

Banks and Building Societies may not accept Direct Debit Instructions for some types of account

MEMBER ENQUIRIES — 0116 284 5390

About The BMF

History

In 1960, incensed by a number of (admittedly) bad accidents and exaggerated reports of leather-jacketed hooligans racing around the streets, the tabloid press started a campaign denigrating motorcycles and the people who rode them. In response to an additional threat from the Cronin Bill in Parliament, a group of like-minded enthusiasts recognised that strength could be gained in numbers. Comprising of members of the bigger motorcycle clubs, they decided to form the Federation of National One Make Clubs (FNOMCC) in early 1961. It didn't exactly trip off the tongue, but it was a start. Heartened by early successes, the organisation quickly expanded to encompass a majority of motorcyclists and in 1965 was renamed the British Motorcyclists Federation. The following three decades has seen the BMF grow in size and stature. In that time, the Federation's activities and political lobbying has achieved many notable successes. These include the introduction of its own motorcycle insurance scheme, which offered a 30 percent no-claims bonus at a time when riders would be lucky to get 10 percent from other insurers. In addition, the present BMF Rider Training Scheme was introduced in 1982 and represents a justifiably proud achievement.

Organisation

Membership

Membership of the BMF is divided into the following categories:

Full (Individual) Membership – Anyone can apply to join the BMF as a full member. Full membership entitles the holder to all the services and benefits provided by the BMF, including single voting rights at the appropriate annual regional meeting and the BMF AGM. A subscription to Motorcycle Rider magazine is also included.

Affiliate Membership – Motorcycle clubs and other organisations with an interest in motorcycling can apply to be affiliated to the BMF. Each club is allocated an appropriate number of votes which can be cast at the specific Annual Regional Meeting, or Clubs Forum; and the BMF AGM. Affiliate status is granted to members of an affiliated club and enables access to BMF benefits and services.

Associate Membership – Similar to Affiliate Membership but without voting rights.

LATEST NEWS AND INFO — BMF.CO.UK

Membership fees and structure

The fee for full membership of the BMF is based on the cost of providing various services. A sliding scale of fees is set for affiliated clubs which also reflects the cost of providing each club with a basic service.

Annual General Meeting

The AGM is open to all full, BMF members who each have one vote. Affiliated clubs can send nominees (members) to the AGM to cast votes on its behalf.

Business of the AGM – The business of the AGM includes the following (as required):
– election of the BMF Management Team
– ratification of BMF Council members elected at regional meetings and Clubs Forum
– election of the Chairman of the Disciplinary Committee
– presentation of Federation accounts
– presentation of motions and constitutional changes
– any other business appropriate to an AGM

BMF Management Team

The BMF Management Team comprises of the Chairman and seven portfolio managers, encompassing: Administration, Finance, Marketing, Political & Technical Services, Affiliate Member Services, Individual Member Services and Public Relations & Communications. The Chairman, Administration, Finance and Marketing managers are directors of BMF (Enterprises) Ltd and administer the legal, business and financial affairs of the Federation.

Annual Regional Meetings

All regions hold an Annual Regional Meeting which is open to full members who reside in the region, and to nominees of any of the region's affiliated clubs. The purpose of the meetings is to elect a Regional Chairman and members of the BMF Council; receive reports on local and national issues from the region's team of volunteers; discuss proposed motions from members and clubs within the region for submission to the AGM, and any other business. Other meetings may be held during the year to discuss items of local interest to the region's members and clubs.

National and One-Make Clubs Forum

The forum convenes an annual meeting for affiliated national clubs which is equal in status and purpose to that of annual regional meetings. Other meetings (for national affiliated clubs) may be held under the auspices of the NOMC Chairman to discuss matters of interest to the clubs.

The BMF Council

The BMF Council meets three times annually and consists of the BMF Management Team and councillors elected at Annual Regional Meetings and the National Clubs Forum. The purpose of the Council is to formulate the BMF's plan of action, monitor policy and progress, and discuss reports from the management team. The BMF Council has authority to form subcommittees to implement council business and assist the management team. Members of the Council are also guarantee holders for BMF (Enterprises) Ltd and represent the interests of the Federation's members in the running of the company.

MEMBER ENQUIRIES – 0116 284 53 90

Keep your distance

We all know the need to see problems before they develop. One of the biggest problems and one of the easiest to fix is to give yourself space. Most riders (and drivers) follow too close. Thus their main attention is on the vehicle ahead because their main worry is not running into the back of it - check to see if you instinctively brake when the driver ahead does - if you do, you are too close. Drop back and you'll find you can look beyond and react to hazards before the driver ahead of you is even aware of them.

Remember to signal

Try to see the road ahead through other road-users' eyes. When signalling and positioning, think what information you can give. Ask yourself what signals you would like to see yourself. Remember that a signal on your part does not give you right of way. Signals can be misunderstood or simply not seen in low sun - consider reinforcing indicators with an arm signal.

Beware of road surfaces

Changing our position in the road is an important part of safe riding. We should be trying to minimise danger by keeping away from it, or splitting the difference if there is more than one hazard to deal with. Only when we can see the hazard can we decide where to put the bike for safety. Remember that the surface becomes important when you need to make machine inputs such as braking, steering or accelerating, and that a view of a bend or a roundabout rarely reveals the state of the road surface until the last moment.

Expect the unexpected

A key factor in riding safely is to ask yourself not only what other road users around you are likely to do, but to have in mind what they might do unexpectedly. Most bike accidents happen because the rider assumed that things would work out... and things didn't go as expected.   The more you think about what might go wrong, the safer you'll be.

Get in gear

It's a very good idea to approach junctions at a speed and in a gear that will allow the rider to pass through the danger zone without delay, and to change speed if necessary without the need for a gear change. Try to keep the engine in the zone where it responds without hesitation in either direction. This usually means running a lower gear than most riders normally use.

1to**1** motorcycle training

Martin Lambert • Senior Instructor • Tel 01452 531103 • Mobile 07831 165786
4 Robert Raikes Avenue • Tuffley • Gloucester • GL4 0QG • www.1to1motorcycletraining.co.uk

Page/Ref		Town	Name	Telephone No.
43	D3	Amesbury	Phoenix Motorcycle Training	01747 873153
38	B4	Barnstaple	5 Star Motorcycle Training	01271 342160
38	B4	Barnstaple	Prodrive the Driver Trainers Ltd	01271 377999
38	B4	Barnstaple	Rob Reed Training	01271 321832
41	G1	Bath	Motag Motorcycle Training	0800 6520677
41	G1	Bath	MotoXp	01225 444127
41	F2	Near Bath	2 Wheel Training	01225 462098
35	G2	Blandford Forum	Maverick Motorcycle Training	01258 821036
36	B3	Bournemouth	A2B School of Motorcycling	0800 0280734
36	B3	Bournemouth	ACE Motorcycle Training	01425 461403
36	A3	Bournemouth	Dorset & Wessex Motorcycle Training	01202 573869
36	A3	Bournemouth	Let's Ride!	0800 6528774
36	A3	Bournemouth	PAS School of Motorcycling	01202 535880
44	D5	Bristol	ACE Motorcycle Training	01179 721333
45	D4	Bristol	Cotswold Motorcycle Training	0800 1978850
41	F1	Bristol	Kickstart Motorcycle Training	0800 0198919
40	C2	Burnham on Sea	A+ Motorcycle Training	01278 788864
30	C5	Camelford	OYB Motorcycle Training	01840 212962
41	F4	Castle Cary	CC Rider Training	01963 351292
45	G5	Chippenham	Phoenix Motorcycle Training	01747 873153
46	A2	Cirencester	Gloucestershire Rider Training	07714 426225
40	D1	Clevedon	In-Gear (UK) Motorcycle Training School	01275 371278
33	E2	Cullompton	KS Advanced Training	01884 829067
35	E4	Dorchester	Nick's Motorcycle Training	01305 854128
35	E3	Dorchester	SJR Motorcycle Training	01305 259778
33	D4	Exeter	Dave Hart Training	01297 22111
32	D4	Exeter	Think Motorcycle & BSW	01392 216021
42	A2	Frome	Roadwise Training	01934 710352
45	F1	Gloucester	Acer Motorcycle Training	01452 720975
44	D4	Hambrook	Bristol Motorcycle Training Centre	01454 776333
40	C3	Highbridge	A+ Motorcycle Training	01278 788864
34	A1	Ilminster	Andy's Motorcycle Training	01460 53053
36	C3	New Milton	Ask The Licence Centre	01258 881012
29	E1	Newton Abbot	Pro Rider Motorcycle Training	01626 336699
24	B3	Penzance	Cornwall Bike Training	01736 333226
28	A3	Plymouth	Damerells Motorcycles	01752 667806
28	B3	Plymouth	Surepass Rider Training	01752 301313
36	B3	Poole	A2B School of Motorcycling	0800 0280734
36	A3	Poole	Motag Motorcycle Training	0800 6520677
36	A3	Poole	Poole Bike Training	01202 330378
36	A3	Poole	Riders 1st Choice Ltd	01202 777136
36	A3	Poole	The Licence Centre	01258 881012
45	F1	Quedgeley	Acer Motorcycle Training	01452 720975
42	D5	Salisbury	A1 Roadcraft Centre	0800 716156
42	D4	Salisbury	Motag Motorcycle Training	0800 6520677
42	B5	Salisbury	Phoenix Motorcycle Training	01747 873153
46	B3	Swindon	Abbey Rider Training	01793 705905
46	B4	Swindon	Motag Motorcycle Training	0800 6520677
46	B5	Swindon	Riding In Action	0870 0201700
33	G1	Taunton	PRIDE	01823 279165
33	G1	Taunton	Taunton School of Motorcycling	01823 354288
45	F1	Tuffley	1 to 1 Motorcycle Training	01452 531103
35	G4	Wareham	Ask The Licence Centre	01258 881012
36	A3	Wareham	Dorset & Wessex Motorcycle Training	01202 573869
41	E3	Wells	Mendip Motorcycle Training	01458 830335
40	C1	Weston-super-Mare	Motag Motorcycle Training	0800 6520677
40	C1	Weston-super-Mare	Road to Freedom Motorcycle and Scooter Training	07884 138 956
35	D4	Weymouth	Karen's Motorcycle Training School	01305 750515
35	D5	Weymouth	Wessex Riders	01305 785672
36	A3	Wimborne Minster	Ask The Licence Centre	01258 881012
36	A2	Wimborne Minster	Wimborne Motorcycle Training	01202 842353
34	B1	Near Yeovil	AEP Motorcycle Training	01935 824891

BRIDGESTONE
PASSION for EXCELLENCE

CIRCUIT TO STREET...
...AND BACK

The latest Battlax is here, the BT-002 Racing Street is designed to compliment the lightest, fastest and best handling sports bikes that money can buy. To give you the confidence to place the bike into a corner with precision and get on the power earlier.

A dual compound front gives rock solid stability and amazing feel when pushing hard into a deep corner while the patented HTSPC construction of the rear combined with an ultra high grip compound ensures that getting to the next corner is fully under your control.

With more than a little help from our MotoGP programme the BT-002 Racing Street has been developed for you to enjoy on the road or to take home to the circuit on your next track day.

Our technology for you to enjoy-so enjoy.

www.bridgestone-eu.com

BATTLAX
BT-002
RACING STREET

Interphone

- the 'must have' Bluetooth helmet communicator

Whether you're new to motorcycling, an experienced long-distance tourer, or a 'born again' sportsbiker, you will have wondered about the possibilities of communicating with others whilst on the move.

Wired intercoms have been available for many years, and can provide effective rider-to-pillion interaction. The more sophisticated versions can also attach to mobile phones and radios, providing longer-range communication. The downside is the cost and complexity of all of those interconnectors, especially when exposed to the elements and rough handling on a motorcycle.

Imagine if you could achieve all of this with a self-contained wireless unit that simply attaches to any kind of helmet in minutes and gives fantastic audio performance. Through the technical mystery of 'Bluetooth' this is now possible.

Based on a specification for *'the world's best motorcycle intercom'*, *Interphone* is the world's first *Bluetooth* intercom with all these features:

- ☼ Bluetooth® Wireless Technology (secure, one-to-one, encrypted channels)
- ☼ Hands-free Phone Operation - using voice dialling capability of phone
- ☼ Voice Activation of Phone - for answering on the move
- ☼ Bluetooth® Intercom - Rider-Pillion or Bike-to-Bike (typically over 150 metres, up to 500 metres)
- ☼ GPS compatible - listen to your GPS directions
- ☼ Full-duplex communication with DSP and noise filtering - natural 2-way conversation
- ☼ Microphone with anti-wind & anti-noise filter
- ☼ Automatic volume control - according to speed and background noise
- ☼ 'Turbo' setting - for noisy applications
- ☼ Excellent performance to over 70 mph
- ☼ Waterproof
- ☼ Rechargeable Lithium battery - giving up to 7 hours talk time (charger included)
- ☼ 12 Month 'no-quibble' Warranty
- ☼ 2 mounting brackets - to suit any helmet

And, whilst we don't endorse the use of a mobile phone when riding, it's astonishingly useful to be able to stop to make a quick call without having to remove helmet and gloves.

The benefits of a full-duplex wireless intercom to your pillion are pretty obvious, but the facility to clearly warn your riding buddy about a road hazard or that you're lost or need petrol is a real boon.

Interphone now provides a solution for those who thought motorcycle intercoms were a nuisance and a waste of time.

At £149.99 each (or £275 for a pair) 'Interphone' is available from all good dealers, or online at www.nitro-helmets.com and www.ogk-shop.com

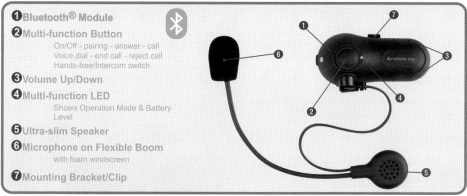

❶ Bluetooth® Module

❷ Multi-function Button
On/Off - pairing - answer - call
Voice dial - end call - reject call
Hands-free/Intercom switch

❸ Volume Up/Down

❹ Multi-function LED
Shows Operation Mode & Battery Level

❺ Ultra-slim Speaker

❻ Microphone on Flexible Boom
with foam windscreen

❼ Mounting Bracket/Clip

For more information contact Moto Comp on:
Tel: 08700-340 283   email: interphone@motocomp.com   Web: www.motocomp.com

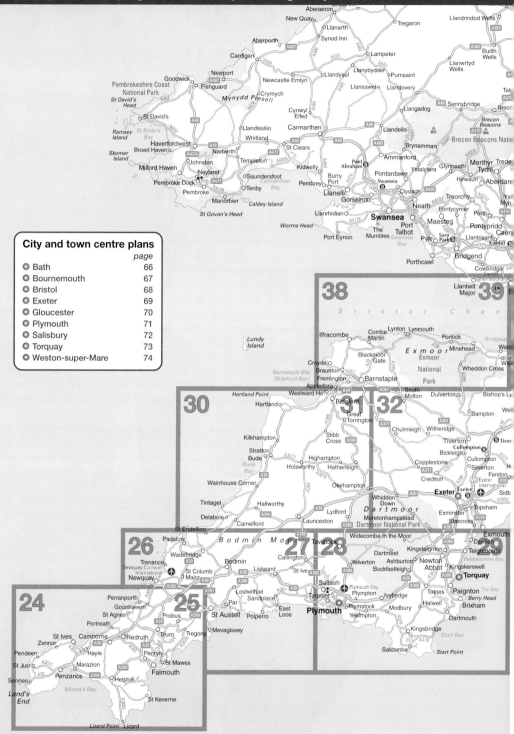

City and town centre plans

Scale 1:1,333,333

0   10   20 miles
0   10   20   30 km

21 miles to 1 inch / 13.3 km to 1 cm

Road maps

Exciting route	Scenic route
Rural route	Coastal route
M5 Motorway	Railway line / station / tunnel
M6Toll Toll motorway	South West Coast Path National Trail / Long Distance Route
Motorway junction with full / limited access (in congested areas there is just a numbered symbol)	Fixed safety camera sites / fixed average speed safety camera sites
Maidstone / Birch / Sarn Motorway service area with off road / full / limited access	Airport with / without scheduled services
A39 Primary route dual / single carriageway	(H) Heliport
24 hour service area on primary route	Built up area
Truro Primary route destination Primary route destinations are places of major traffic importance linked by the primary route network. They are shown on a green background on direction signs.	Town / Village / Other settlement
A39 'A' road dual / single carriageway	**Hythe** Seaside destination
B/403 'B' road dual / single carriageway	National boundary
Minor road	**DEVON** County / Unitary Authority boundary and name
Road with restricted access	Heritage Coast
Roads with passing places	468 ▲941 Spot / Summit height (in metres)
Road proposed or under construction	National Park
Multi-level junction with full / limited access (with junction number)	Woodland
Roundabout	Danger Zone Military range
4 Road distance in miles between markers	Lake / Dam / River / Waterfall
Road tunnel	Canal / Dry canal / Canal tunnel
Steep hill (arrows point downhill)	Lighthouse
Toll Level crossing / Toll	Beach
St. Malo 8hrs Car ferry route with journey times	

Tourist information centre (open all year)	Distillery	Nature reserve (NNR indicates a National Nature Reserve)
Tourist information centre (open seasonally)	Ecclesiastical building	Racecourse
Ancient monument	Event venue	Rail Freight Terminal
Aquarium	Farm park	Ski slope (artificial / natural)
Aqueduct / Viaduct	Garden	Spotlight nature reserve (Best sites for access to nature)
Arboretum	Golf course	Steam railway centre / Preserved railway
Battlefield	Historic house	Surfing beach
Blue flag beach	Historic ship	Theme park
Camp site / Caravan site	Major football club	University
Castle	Major shopping centre / Outlet village	Vineyard
Cave	Major sports venue	Wildlife park / Zoo
Country park	Motor racing circuit	Other interesting feature
County cricket ground	Museum / Art gallery	National Trust

These symbols appear on road maps and town plans

			Rider recommended
Motorcycle training	A & E Hospitals	Restaurants
Dealerships	Bike friendly accommodation	Bars
Dealerships and Servicing	Club meets	Cafés
Servicing only	Petrol Stations in rural areas	Camping

City and town centre plans

M8	Motorway		Motorcycle on-street parking bays
A40	Primary route dual / single carriageway	£	Car park discount to motorcycles
A4119	'A' road dual / single carriageway	F	Car park free to motorcycles
B4632	'B' road dual / single carriageway	P	Standard car park
	Other road dual / single carriageway	WC	Public toilets
	Restricted access street	†	Ecclesiastical building
	Pedestrian street		Tourist information centre (open all year / seasonally)
	Path / Footbridge		Tourist building
	One way street		Higher Education building
	Railway line / station		Hospital
	Light rail station		Other important building
	Bus / coach station	†	Cemetery
			Recreational area / Open space

ISLES OF SCILLY

same scale as main map

Scale 1:253,485

0	2	4	6 miles

| 0 | 2 | 4 | 6 | 8 | 10 km |

4 miles to 1 inch / 2.53 km to 1 cm

A B C D

1

Scale 1:253,485

0　　　　2　　　　4　　　　6 miles
0　　2　　4　　6　　8　　10 km
4 miles to 1 inch / 2.53 km to 1 cm

LUNDY

North
West
Point

Lundy
Heritage Coast

LUNDY

Lundy Island
(NT)

Lundy
NNR

Rat Island

Shutter
Rock

same scale as main map

Hartland
Point

Titchberry

Hartland
Abbey

Hartland
Quay

Stoke　Ha

Milford

Edisto

Elmscott

South Hole

Knaps Longpeak

Welcomb

Mead

Darr
Woo

Gooseham

Ea

2

Morwenstow

Higher
Sharpnose
Point

Shop

Lower
Sharpnose
Point

Woodford

Coombe

Hartland
Heritage Coast

Stibb

A

Stratton

Maer

Poughill

He
Bush

Bude
Haven

Flexbury

Strattc

BUDE BAY

Bude

3

Lynstone

Stratton Museum

Upton

Marhamch

Helebridge

3

A

Widemouth Bay

Box's
Shop

Tits

Coppathorne

Week C

Dizzard Point

Poundstock

Treskinnick Cross

Tregole

Penlean

We
St M

St Gennys

Trewint

Crackington Haven

19

Cambeak

Rosecare

Jacobstow

Crackington

Wainhouse Corner

4

Higher
Whiteleigh

Tresparrett
Posts

Trengune

South Wheatley

Fire Beacon Point

Collamoor
Head

Langdon

Beeny

Canworthy
Water

Marshgate

Tros

Tresparrett

Trelash

Warbstow

Boscastle

Boscastle
Pottery

Lesnewth

Otterham

Trevalga

Auk Walk

Trem

Tintagel
Castle

Hallworthy

Treneglos

Tresn

Tintagel Head

Bossiney

Hendraburnick

Three
Hammers

Tintagel Old Post
Office (NT)

Tintagel

Davidstow

Cold Northcott

11

Badgall

Treknow

Trewarmett

Trewassa

Tremail

Penpethy

Start
Point

Trevivian

St Clether

A195

Trebarwith

Rockhead

Downhead

Laneast

Delabole

Tregunnon

Trewe

5

Trelygga

Camelford

Tregoodwell

New Park

Bowithick

Altarnun

Tredalle

Westdowns

Valley Truckle

Trewalder

Pencarrow

Lower
Moor

Buttern Hill

346

Fivelanes

Trewint

Lanteglos

Tresinney

Rough
Tor

Bray
Down

Newland

Rumps
Point

The Mouls

Port
Quin

Port
Isaac

Helstone

Watergate

400

Brown
Willy

346

Pentire Point

Port Quin
Bay

Port Gaverne

Treveighan

Gam
Tor

New Polzeath

Trelights

St Teath

Pendogg

Tregeare
Rounds

St Teath

Michaelstow

A

26

B

C

27

D

Bournemouth Information

Just mentioning Bournemouth, conjures images of sophistication where the Continent blends effortlessly with contemporary, traditional and everything British.

Photo © Bournemouth Tourism

Renowned for its seven miles of golden beaches, beautiful parks and gardens and with "100 great things to do and sea" in and around the area, Bournemouth ensures you are truly spoilt for choice!

"100 great things to do and sea"

An ideal all year-round resort there's plenty to keep you entertained in every season, whether it is quality attractions, family fun, live entertainment, shopping, water sports, action, adventure, history, heritage or gourmet dining. Kids will love Splashdown, Monkey World, Oceanarium and Adventure Wonderland. Nature lovers will enjoy Brownsea Island and the enchanting New Forest; for history and heritage fans there's the Jurassic Coastline a mind blowing 185 million years of the earth's history in 95 miles of stunning coastline.

There are great visitor attractions in Bournemouth, and the surrounding countryside villages and towns hold some of England's most attractive and alluring museums, galleries and family-themed destinations.

And of course there's Bournemouth's breathtaking seafront with its promenade, pier and golden sand, for sports people this part of Britain is soon to be home to Europe's only artificial surf reef!

Just three miles from Bournemouth Pier, Boscombe beach will soon be at the top of the list of great places to surf when Europe's first artificial surf reef is opened, with scheduled completion September 2007. The reef will be classed as a Grade 5, double the amount of good surfing days and host around 10,000 surf visits per annum.

Bournemouth buzzes by day and night with restaurants, bars, nightclubs and live entertainment venues, and if you're into retail therapy then Bournemouth's dazzling array of shops, from boutique chic to department stores, will keep you busy.

It is true that England has gastronomically evolved to become a country of connoisseurs and Bournemouth is at the forefront of our love affair with food! There's everything on the menu from authentic Lebanese, Latin, Mediterranean and Middle Eastern to the taste of regional Italian cooking, Greek and French as well as good, solid traditional fare, representing the best in British food.

Photo © Bournemouth Tourism

So, Bournemouth has it all, an ideal resort for a truly memorable break!

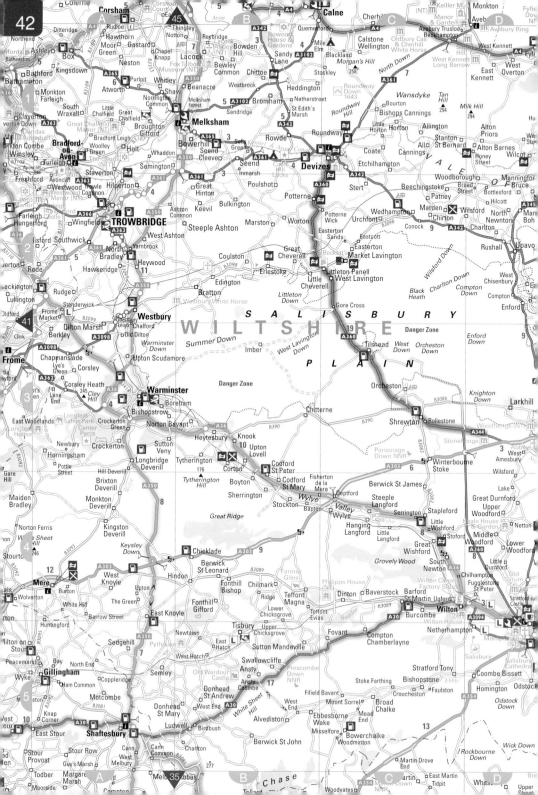

Specialist driving and parking guides

www.thePIEguide.com

London Bike Guide

The essential companion for riders in the capital. This customised street map shows parking rules and concessions for bikers for all 33 London boroughs.

It helps riders by mapping out all dedicated bike bays, colour-coding residents parking to reflect where bikes can park free of charge, and showing all the bays on Red Routes available to riders. It also shows speed cameras, bus lanes and petrol stations.

Since launching in 2002, PIE has built its reputation on helping people find what they are looking for on maps customised especially for them, both in print and online.

We produce quality maps that are tailored to the unique needs of specific driving communities. Our team of surveyors work with these communities to research all our content to make sure it is up to date and of value.

We design and build new symbols for our maps and colour-code them to reflect important parking rules and regulations. We are passionate about quality and getting the best and most relevant data for our customers.

Other PIE Guides

- London Blue Badge Parking Guide
- London Lorry Guide
- UK Blue Badge Road Atlas
- London Van Guide
- London Bike Guide
- Transport Manager's Wall Map
- The South West Bike Guide

www.thePIEguide.com or call 0870 444 5434

Buying a Used Motorcycle? CheckABike can save you time and money.

You've done your research, you know exactly which make and model you want. So now all you need to do is find the right motorcycle for you. But beware, there are hidden pitfalls.

Even the most pristene looking bike could be hiding a darker past. If it has been written off, stolen or still has finance outstanding against it, you could be buying a two wheel horror story!

However, a CheckABike report can help you avoid these pitfalls and with the £30,000 CheckABike Report insurance can help to cut the financial risk of buying a used Bike.

In addition, CheckABike is the only vehicle data check specifically designed for motorcycles with access to the Motorcycle Industry Association's (MCIA) database. This means you'll get a more complete picture of the bike you are looking at.

All our reports will give you the details of your bike's make, model, engine size, colour, date of manufacture and date of first registration. You can also find out if the bike you are looking at was imported from outside the EU.

How Does CheckABike Work?
A Step By Step Guide

Step 1

Register your details with us. It is free to sign up and you will purchase checks when you need them.

Step 2

Decide whether you want to buy CheckABike solo or multi. We would always recommend buying a multi check unless you are certain that you will only be looking at one bike. A CheckABike Multi allows you to check the history for up to 5 vehicles and to register the motorcycle you buy to qualify for our CheckABike Report Insurance.

Step 3

Buy your CheckABike motorcycle history report with your credit or debit card. Once you have paid, you will have 60 days to check your dream machine.

Step 4

Check a motorcycle by entering:

- the Vehicle Registration Mark (VRM)

- the Vehicle Identification Number (VIN or chassis number), don't worry if you don't have it, you can come back with it later

- the approximate current mileage if you know it. This will help us to identify any mileage anomalies for you

You will get the results instantly.

Step 5

Before you buy the vehicle, read our Buying Advice at www.checkabike.co.uk and print off the check list. A CheckABike report can help you make an informed decision, but cannot protect you from every eventuality; by following our advice you will know some of the things to look out for.

Step 6

Confirm the VIN if you have not already done so, before you buy it. The VIN is unique to each motorcycle and is one way of checking that its identity has not been changed fraudulently. It can be found on the V5C and in various places on the bike itself. If you are unsure where to look, contact your local garage/dealer, they should be able to tell you.

Step 7

After you've bought the bike, don't forget to return to the site to register your CheckABike Report Insurance. This policy will cover you for specific financial loss due to the data supplied being incorrect or incomplete.

You can return to the site at any time and log in using your e-mail address and password. Just click on 'View My Checks' and you will be able to see all the checks you have already, or you can click 'Check A Bike' to access further checks. Buying a new motorcycle should be fun, don't let it become a nightmare, check it out with CheckABike. Visit www.checkabike.co.uk to buy a check online.

BUYING A USED BIKE? CHECK IT OUT

With CheckABike you get:
- Instant results online
- Up to £30,000 CheckABike report insurance
- Plus, with CheckABike Multi you can check up to 5 separate bikes for as little as £5 for each bike.

No One Checks More For Less
Our checks were the first checks available to the public which use MCIA (Motor Cycle Industry Association) Data as part of the standard history check.

In partnership with

THE MOTOR CYCLE INDUSTRY ASSOCIATION

www.checkabike.co.uk

CheckABike is provided by Experian Ltd. Experian is an appointed representative of Motorfile Ltd, which is authorised and regulated by the Financial Services Authority. Motorfile Ltd, Talbot House, Talbot Street, Nottingham, NG80 1TH. Registered in England Company No. 3009493. VAT No. 145899025. CheckABike cannot reveal a write off where the motorcycle has been self or third party insured and may not identify 'cloned' or 'ringed' vehicles which are illegal copies of another vehicle bearing both a false Vehicle Registration Mark and Vehicle Identification number. CheckABike insurance is underwritten by Pinnacle Insurance Plc.

If you are unfortunate enough to be involved in a road traffic accident, you should take names, addresses and telephone numbers of the other parties concerned and any witnesses to the accident. Use the form we have supplied on the facing page and complete if possible.

If you have a phone camera try and take photographs of the accident scene, road layout and signs if possible.

It is very important, no matter how minor the accident may be, to report the accident to the police and obtain a police reference number.

If the accident was not your fault then you may be entitled to make a claim against the other party for damages to your motorcycle, personal effects and for any personal injuries you have suffered.

As with all compensation claims, you will need to prove that the other party was responsible for your losses.

If you are intending to claim expenses such as prescription costs or travelling expenses remember to keep receipts as evidence.

It is always sensible to seek medical attention (whether a visit to your GP or A&E) regardless of whether or not you intend to make a claim for personal injury.

If you need some urgent advice please do not hesitate to give us a call - **020 8246 4900.**

Ride On.........

Your **report** guide
obtain as many of the details below or get **someone** to **help** you

Other drivers details

name:

address:

daytime phone:

evening phone:

registration no:

their insurance company:

policy/certificate no:

you must try and get a witness ask them to put their details on this card

Witness 1

name:

address:

phone: email:

Witness 2

name:

address:

phone: email:

RSS... for heavyweight legal expertise
accident forms are online: **www.ridersupport.co.uk**

020 8246 4900
your total accident solution **...ride on**

In this index place and place of interest names are followed by a page number and a grid reference. The place can be found by searching that grid square. Where more than one place has the same name, each can be distinguished by the abbreviated county or unitary authority name shown after the place name. A list of abbreviations used for these names is shown to the right.

Major places of interest are shown within the index in blue type. Postcode information is supplied for places of interest in blue type after the county name.

B. & N.E.Som.	Bath & North East Somerset
Bourne.	Bournemouth
Cornw.	Cornwall
Glos.	Gloucestershire
Hants.	Hampshire
Here.	Herefordshire
I.o.S.	Isles of Scilly
I.o.W.	Isle of Wight
Mon.	Monmouthshire
N.Som.	North Somerset

Oxon.	Oxfordshire
Plym.	Plymouth
S.Glos.	South Gloucestershire
Som.	Somerset
Swin.	Swindon
V. of Glam.	Vale of Glamorgan
W.Berks.	West Berkshire
Wilts.	Wiltshire

A

Abbas Combe 41 G5
Abbots Bickington 31 E2
Abbots Leigh 44 C5
Abbots Worthy 43 G4
Abbotsbury 34 C4
Abbotsbury Swannery
 Dorset DT3 4JG 34 C4
Abbotsham 31 F1
Abbotskerswell 29 E2
Abbotts Ann 43 F3
Abbott's Barton 43 G4
Abbottswood 43 F5
Abenhall 45 D1
Ablington *Glos.* 46 B2
Ablington *Wilts.* 43 D3
Abson 45 E5
Acton 35 G5
Acton Turville 45 F4
Adber 41 E5
Adsborough 33 G1
Adscombe 40 A4
Alice in Wonderland Family
 Park *Dorset* BH23 6BA
 36 B3
Affpuddle 35 F3
Afton 36 D4
Aish *Devon* 28 C2
Aish *Devon* 29 E3
Aisholt 40 A4
Albaston 28 A1
Alcombe 39 F3
Aldbourne 46 C5
Alderbury 43 D5
Alderholt 36 B1
Alderley 45 E3
Alderton 45 F4
Aldsworth 46 B2
Aley 40 A4
Alfardisworthy 31 D2
Alfington 33 F4
Alford 41 F4
Alhampton 41 F4
All Cannings 42 C1
Allaleigh 29 E3
Allbrook 43 G5
Aller 40 D5
Allercombe 33 E4
Allerford *Devon* 31 F5
Allerford *Som.* 39 F3
Allet Common 25 E2
Allington *Dorset* 34 B3
Allington *Wilts.* 43 E4
Allington *Wilts.* 42 C1
Allington *Wilts.* 45 F5
Allowenshay 34 A1
Almer 35 G3
Almiston Cross 31 E1
Almondsbury 44 D4
Alphington 32 D4
Alston 34 A2
Alston Sutton 40 D2
Alstone 40 C3
Alswear 32 B1
Altarnun 30 D5
Alton Barnes 42 D1
Alton Pancras 35 E2
Alton Priors 42 D1
Alvediston 42 B3
Alverdiscott 31 G1
Alvescot 46 C2
Alveston 44 D4

Alvington 44 D2
Alweston 35 D1
Alwington 31 F1
Amalebra 24 B3
Amberley 45 F2
Amesbury 43 D3
Ameysford 36 A2
Ampfield 43 F5
Ampney Crucis 46 A2
Ampney St. Mary 46 A2
Ampney St. Peter 46 A2
Amport 43 F3
Andersea 40 C4
Andersfield 40 B4
Anderson 35 F3
Andover 43 F3
Andover Down 43 F3
Andoversford 46 A1
Angarrack 24 C3
Angarrick 25 E3
Anna Valley 43 F3
Ansford 41 F4
Ansty 42 B5
Ansty Coombe 42 B5
Ansty Cross 35 E2
Antony 27 G3
Anvil Corner 31 E3
Appledore *Devon* 38 A4
Appledore *Devon* 33 E2
Appleshaw 43 F3
Appley 33 E1
Arlingham 45 E1
Arlington *Devon* 38 C3
Arlington *Glos.* 46 B2
Arlington Beccott 38 C3
Arne 35 G4
Arnolfini Gallery *Bristol*
 BS1 4QA 68 C1
Ascott d'Oyley 46 D1
Ascott Earl 46 C1
Ascott-under-
 Wychwood 46 D1
Ash *Dorset* 35 F1
Ash *Som.* 41 D5
Ash Barton 31 G3
Ash Bullayne 32 B3
Ash Mill 32 B1
Ash Priors 33 F1
Ash Thomas 33 E2
Ashbrittle 33 E1
Ashburton 29 D2
Ashbury *Devon* 31 G4
Ashbury *Oxon.* 46 C4
Ashcombe *Devon* 29 F1
Ashcombe *N.Som.* 40 C1
Ashcott 40 D4
Ashford *Devon* 28 C4
Ashford *Devon* 38 B4
Ashford *Hants.* 36 B1
Ashill *Devon* 33 E2
Ashill *Som.* 34 A1
Ashington 41 E5
Ashley *Devon* 32 A2
Ashley *Glos.* 45 G3
Ashley *Hants.* 43 F4
Ashley *Hants.* 36 C3
Ashley *Wilts.* 42 A1
Ashley Down 44 C5
Ashley Heath 36 B2
Ashmansworth 43 G2
Ashmansworthy 31 E2
Ashmore 35 G1
Ashprington 29 E3

Ashreigney 32 A2
Ashton *Cornw.* 24 D4
Ashton *Cornw.* 27 G2
Ashton Common 42 A2
Ashton Court Estate *N.Som.*
 BS41 9JN 44 C5
Ashton Keynes 46 A3
Ashurst 36 D1
Ashurst Bridge 36 D1
Ashwater 31 E4
Ashwick 41 F3
Askerswell 34 C3
Asthall 46 C1
Asthall Leigh 46 D1
Aston 46 D2
At-Bristol *Bristol*
 BS1 5DB 68 C1
Athelhampton 35 E3
Athelney 40 C5
Atherington 31 G1
Atworth 42 A1
Aughton 43 E2
Aunk 33 E3
Aust 44 C4
Avebury 46 B5
Avebury Trusloe 42 C1
Avening 45 F2
Aveton Gifford 28 C4
Avington 43 F1
Avon 36 B3
Avoncliff 42 A2
Avonmouth 44 C5
Avonwick 28 D3
Awbridge 43 F5
Awkley 44 C4
Awliscombe 33 F3
Awre 45 E2
Axbridge 40 D2
Axford 46 C5
Axminster 33 G4
Axmouth 33 G4
Axtown 28 B2
Aylburton 44 D2
Aylesbeare 33 E4
Ayshford 33 E2

B

Babbacombe 29 F2
Babbacombe Model Village
 Torbay TQ1 3LA 29 F2
Babcary 41 E5
Babeny 28 C1
Backwell 41 D1
Badbury 46 B4
Badbury Wick 46 B4
Badgall 30 D5
Badgeworth 45 G1
Badgworth 40 C2
Badminton 45 F4
Badworthy 28 C2
Bagber 35 E1
Bagendon 46 A2
Bagley 41 D3
Bagnor 43 G1
Bagpath 45 F3
Bagshot 43 F1
Bagstone 45 D4
Baldhu 25 E2
Ball Hill 43 G1
Ball's Green 45 F3

Balmerlawn 36 D2
Baltonsborough 41 E4
Bampton *Devon* 33 D1
Bampton *Oxon.* 46 D2
Bank 36 C2
Bankland 40 C5
Bantham 28 C4
Banwell 40 C2
Bapton 42 B4
Bar End 43 G5
Barbrook 38 D3
Barford St. Martin 42 C4
Barne Barton 28 A3
Barnsley 46 A2
Barnstaple 38 B4
Barnwood 45 F1
Barr 33 F1
Barrington 34 A1
Barripper 24 D3
Barrow *Som.* 41 G4
Barrow *Som.* 41 E3
Barrow Gurney 41 D1
Barrow Street 42 A4
Barry 40 A1
Barry Island Pleasure Park
 V. of Glam. CF62 5TR 40 A1
Bartley 36 D1
Barton 29 F2
Barton End 45 F3
Barton on Sea 36 C3
Barton St. David 41 E4
Barton Stacey 43 G3
Barton Town 38 C3
Barwick 34 C1
Bashley 36 C3
Bason Bridge 40 C3
Basset's Cross 31 G3
Batch 40 C2
Batcombe *Dorset* 34 D2
Batcombe *Som.* 41 F4
Bath 41 G1
Bath Abbey *B. & N.E.Som.*
 BA1 1LT 66 B2
Bath Spa Project
 B. & N.E.Som. BA1 1SJ 66 B2
Bathampton 41 G1
Bathealton 33 E1
Batheaston 41 G1
Bathford 41 G1
Bathpool *Cornw.* 27 F1
Bathpool *Som.* 33 G1
Bathway 41 E2
Batson 28 D5
Battisborough Cross 28 C4
Battleton 32 D1
Battramsley 36 D3
Baulking 46 D3
Baunton 46 A2
Baverstock 42 C4
Bawdrip 40 C4
Bay 42 A5
Baydon 46 C5
Bayford 41 G5
Beach 45 E5
Beachley 44 C3
Beacon *Devon* 33 F3
Beacon *Devon* 33 G3
Beacon Hill 35 G2
Beaford 31 G2
Bealsmill 27 G1
Beaminster 34 B2
Beanacre 42 B1
Beardon 31 G5

Beare 33 D3
Bearwood 36 A3
Beaworthy 31 F4
Beckhampton 42 C1
Beckington 42 A2
Bedchester 35 F1
Bedminster 44 C5
Beechingstoke 42 C2
Beeny 30 C4
Beer 33 G5
Beer Hackett 34 D1
Beercrocombe 40 C5
Beesands 29 E4
Beeson 29 E4
Beetham 33 G2
Beggearn Huish 39 G4
Beili-glas 44 A2
Belchalwell 35 E2
Belchalwell Street 35 E2
Bellever 28 C1
Belluton 41 F1
Belowda 26 C2
Belsford 29 D3
Belstone 32 A4
Belstone Corner 32 A4
Bemerton 42 D4
Bennacott 31 D4
Bentham 45 G1
Benton 38 C4
Benville Lane 34 C2
Bere Alston 28 A2
Bere Ferrers 28 A2
Bere Regis 35 F3
Berepper 25 D4
Berkeley 45 D3
Berkley 42 A3
Berriowbridge 27 F1
Berrow 40 B2
Berry Cross 31 F2
Berry Down Cross 38 B3
Berry Hill 44 C1
Berry Pomeroy 29 E2
Berrynarbor 38 B3
Berwick Bassett 46 B5
Berwick St. James 42 C4
Berwick St. John 42 B5
Berwick St. Leonard 42 B4
Bettiscombe 34 A3
Bettws Newydd 44 A2
Beverstone 45 F3
Bevington 45 D3
Bewley Common 42 B1
Bibury 46 B2
Bickenhall 33 G2
Bickerton 29 E5
Bickham 39 F3
Bickham Bridge 28 D3
Bickham House 32 D5
Bickington *Devon* 38 B4
Bickington *Devon* 29 D1
Bickleigh *Devon* 28 B2
Bickleigh *Devon* 32 D3
Bickleton 38 B4
Bicknoller 40 A4
Bickton 36 B1
Bicton Park Gardens *Devon*
 EX9 7BJ 33 E5
Biddestone 45 F5
Biddisham 40 C2
Bideford 31 F1
Bidlake 31 F5
Big Sheep, The
 Devon EX39 5AP 31 F1
Bigbury 28 C4

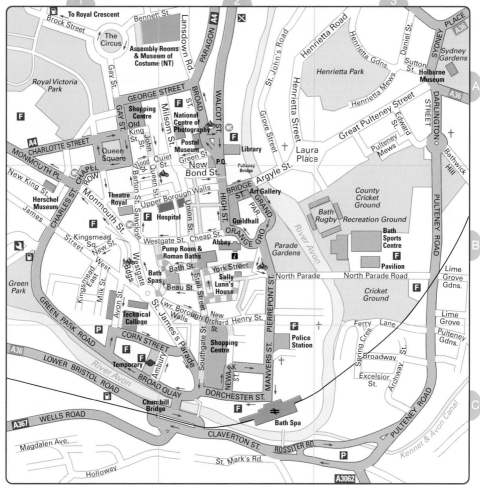

0   200 yds

0   200m

See page 23 for key to map symbols

ⓘ Tourist Information
Abbey Chambers, Abbey
Churchyard, Bath, BA1 1LY
Tel: 0906 711 2000

Ⓗ Hospital A & E
Royal United Hospital,
Combe Park, Bath, BA1 3NG
Tel: 01225 428331

Ⓟ Resident Parking Rules:
Motorcyclists park for free

Ⓟ Pay & Display Bays:
Motorcycles free

Bus Lanes:
Not permitted to motorcycles

Ⓟ Local Parking Contact:
Tel: 01225 477133

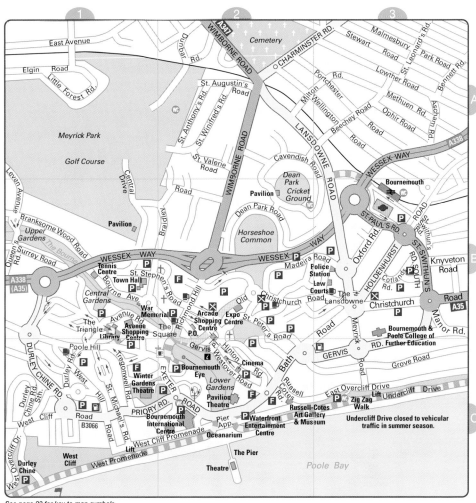

0 400 yds
0 400m

See page 23 for key to map symbols

Tourist Information
Westover Road,
Bournemouth, BH1 2BU
Tel: 0845 05 11 700

Hospital A & E
Royal Bournemouth Hospital,
Castle Lane East, Bournemouth,
BH7 7DW Tel: 01202 303626

Resident Parking Rules:
Permit required for
motorcycles

Pay & Display Bays:
Motorcyclists have to pay

Bus Lanes:
Not permitted to motorcycles

Local Parking Contact:
Tel: 01202 454721

0 | 200 yds
0 | 200m

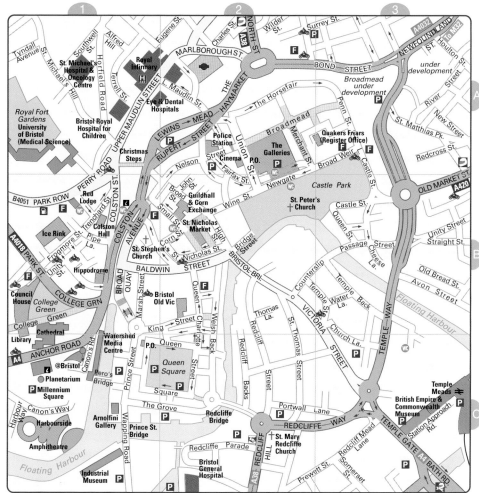

See page 23 for key to map symbols

i Tourist Information
The Annexe, Wildscreen Walk,
Harbourside, Bristol, BS1 5DB
Tel: 0906 711 2191

H Hospital A & E
Bristol Royal Infirmary,
Marlborough Street, Bristol,
BS2 8HW **Tel: 0117 923 0000**

P Resident Parking Rules:
Permit required for
motorcycles

P Pay & Display Bays:
Motorcyclists have to pay

Bus Lanes:
Motorcycles permitted

P Local Parking Contact:
Tel: 0117 922 2198

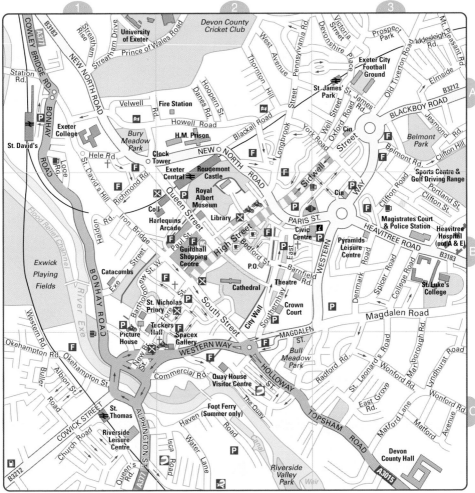

See page 23 for key to map symbols

Tourist Information
Civic Centre, Paris Street, Exeter, EX1 1JJ
Tel: 01392 265700

Hospital A & E
Royal Devon & Exeter Hospital (Wonford), Barrack Road, Exeter, EX2 5DW Tel: 01392 411611

Resident Parking Rules: Motorcyclists park for free

Pay & Display Bays: Motorcycles free

Bus Lanes: Not permitted to motorcycles

Local Parking Contact: Tel: 0845 155 1004

0			500 yds
0			500m

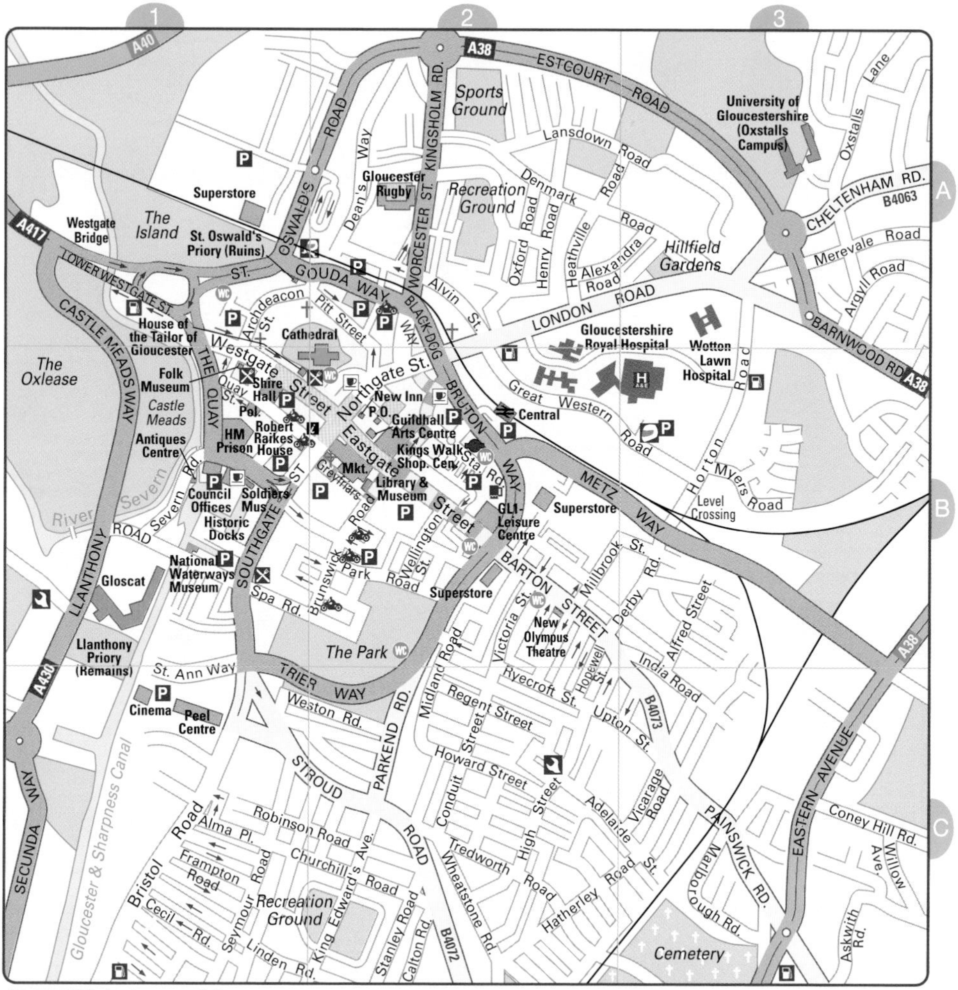

See page 23 for key to map symbols

Adelaide Street	C2	Great Western Road	B2	Pitt Street	A2
Alexandra Road	A2	Greyfriars	B2	Quay Street	B1
Alfred Street	B3	Hatherley Road	C2	Regent Street	C2
Alma Place	C1	Heathville Road	A2	Robinson Road	C1
Alvin Street	A2	Henry Road	A2	Ryecroft Street	C2
Archdeacon Street	A1	High Street	C2	St. Ann Way	C1
Argyll Road	A3	Hopewell Street	C2	St. Oswald's Road	A1
Askwith Road	C3	Horton Road	B3	Secunda Way	C1
Barnwood Road	A3	Howard Street	C2	Severn Road	B1
Barton Street	B2	India Road	B3	Seymour Road	C1
Black Dog Way	A2	King Edward's Avenue	C2	Southgate Street	B1
Bristol Road	C1	Kingsholm Road	A2	Spa Road	B1
Brunswick Road	B2	Lansdown Road	A2	Stanley Road	C2
Bruton Way	B2	Linden Road	C1	Station Road	B2
Calton Road	C2	Llanthony Road	B1	Stroud Road	C1
Castle Meads Way	A1	London Road	A2	The Quay	B1
Cecil Road	C1	Lower Westgate Street	A1	Tredworth Road	C2
Cheltenham Road	A3	Marlborough Road	C3	Trier Way	C1
Churchill Road	C1	Merevale Road	A3	Upton Street	C2
Conduit Street	C2	Metz Way	B2	Vicarage Road	C3
Coney Hill Road	C3	Midland Road	C2	Victoria Street	B2
Dean's Way	A2	Millbrook Street	B2	Wellington Street	B2
Denmark Road	A2	Myers Road	B3	Westgate Street	A1
Derby Road	B2	Northgate Street	B2	Weston Road	C1
Estcourt Road	A2	Oxford Road	A2	Wheatstone Road	C2
Eastern Avenue	C3	Oxstalls Lane	A3	Willow Avenue	C3
Eastgate Street	B2	Painswick Road	C3	Worcester Street	A2
Frampton Road	C1	Park Road	B2		
Gouda Way	A1	Parkend Road	C2		

_i_ Tourist Information
28 Southgate Street,
Gloucester, GL1 2DP
Tel: 01452 421188

H Hospital A & E
Gloucester Royal Hospital,
Great Western Rd, Gloucester,
GL1 3NN **Tel: 08454 222 222**

P Resident Parking Rules:
Permit required for
motorcycles

P Pay & Display Bays:
Motorcyclists have to pay

Bus Lanes:
Not permitted to motorcycles

P Local Parking Contact:
Tel: 01452 396723

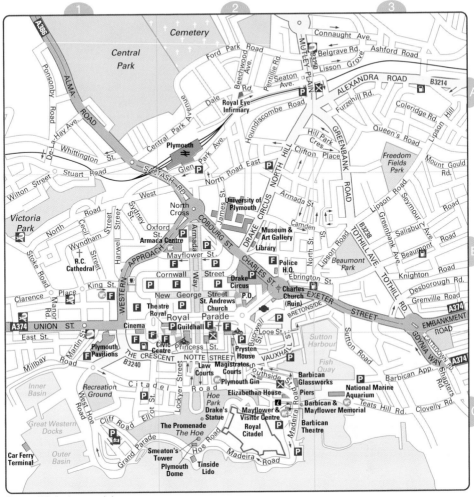

See page 23 for key to map symbols

Tourist Information
Plymouth Mayflower Centre,
3-5 The Barbican, PL1 2LR
Tel: 01752 306 330

Hospital A & E
Derriford Hospital, Derriford Rd,
Crownhill, Plymouth, PL6 8DH
Tel: 0845 155 8155

Resident Parking Rules:
Permit required for
motorcycles

Pay & Display Bays:
Motorcycles free

Bus Lanes:
Not permitted to motorcycles

Local Parking Contact:
Tel: 01752 304021

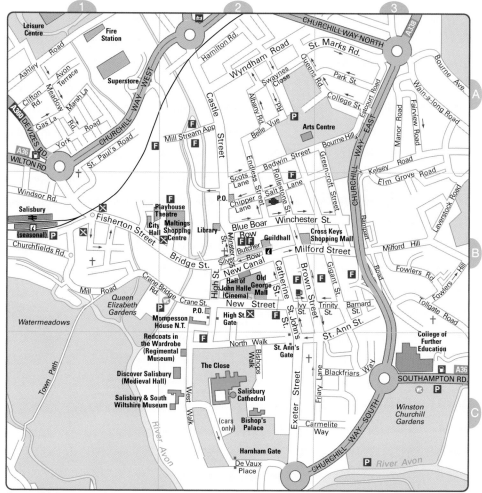

See page 23 for key to map symbols

Tourist Information
Fish Row, Salisbury,
SP1 1EJ
Tel: 01722 334956

Hospital A & E
Salisbury District Hospital,
Odstock Road, Salisbury,
SP2 8BJ Tel: 01722 336262

Resident Parking Rules:
Permit required for
motorcycles

Pay & Display Bays:
Motorcyclists have to pay

Bus Lanes:
Not permitted to motorcycles

Local Parking Contact:
Tel: 01722 434326

0 400 yds
0 400m

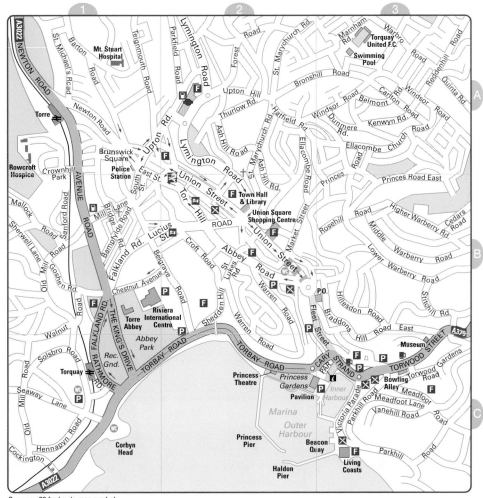

See page 23 for key to map symbols

ℹ Tourist Information
Vaughan Parade, Torquay,
TQ2 5JG
Tel: 0870 70 70 010

Ⓗ Hospital A & E
Torbay District General Hospital,
Newton Road, Torquay,
TQ2 7AA Tel: 01803 614567

Ⓟ Resident Parking Rules:
Motorcyclists park for free

Ⓟ Pay & Display Bays:
Motorcyclists have to pay

Bus Lanes:
Not permitted to motorcycles

Ⓟ Local Parking Contact:
Tel: 01803 207695

0   400 yds
0   400m

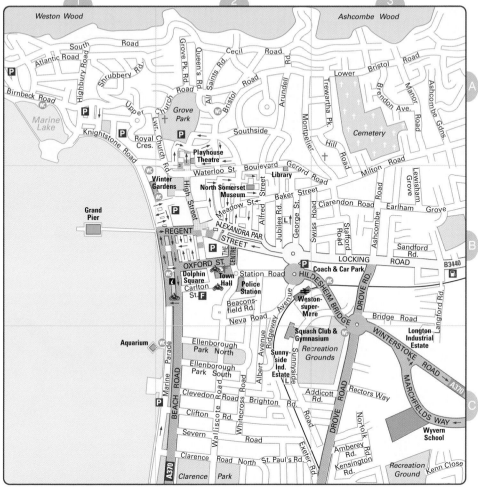

See page 23 for key to map symbols

Addicott Road	C2	Ellenborough Park North	C2	Norfolk Road	C3	
Albert Avenue	C2	Ellenborough Park South	C2	Oxford Street	B2	
Alexandra Parade	B2	Exeter Road	C2	Queen's Road	A2	
Alfred Street	B2	George Street	B2	Rectors Way	C3	
All Saints Road	A2	Gerard Road	A2	Regent Street	B2	
Amberey Road	C3	Grove Park Road	A2	Ridgeway Avenue	C2	
Arundell Road	A2	High Street	B2	Royal Crescent	A1	
Ashcombe Gardens	A3	Highbury Road	A1	St. Paul's Road	C2	
Ashcombe Road	B3	Hildesheim Bridge	B2	Sandford Road	B3	
Atlantic Road	A1	Hill Road	A3	Severn Road	C2	
Baker Street	B2	Jubilee Road	B2	Shrubbery Road	A1	
Beach Road	C2	Kenn Close	C3	South Road	A1	
Beaconsfield Road	B2	Kensington Road	C3	Southside	A2	
Birnbeck Road	A1	Knightstone Road	A1	Stafford Road	B3	
Brendon Avenue	A3	Langford Road	B3	Station Road	B2	
Bridge Road	B3	Lewisham Grove	B3	Sunnyside Road	C2	
Brighton Road	C2	Locking Road	B3	Swiss Road	B3	
Bristol Road	A2	Lower Bristol Road	A3	The Centre	B2	
Carlton Street	B2	Lower Church Road	A1	Trewartha Park	A3	
Cecil Road	A2	Manor Road	A3	Upper Church Road	A1	
Clarence Road North	C2	Marchfields Way	C3	Walliscote Road	C2	
Clarendon Road	B3	Marine Parade	C2	Waterloo Street Boulevard	B2	
Clevedon Road	C2	Meadow Street	B2	Whitecross Road	C2	
Clifton Road	C2	Milton Road	B3	Winterstoke Road	C3	
Drove Road	C3	Montpelier	A2			
Earlham Grove	B3	Neva Road	B2			

i Tourist Information
Beach Lawns,
Weston-super-Mare, BS23 1AT
Tel: 01934 888800

H Hospital A & E
Weston General Hospital,
Grange Rd, Uphill,
BS23 4TQ   Tel: 01934 636363

P Resident Parking Rules:
Permit required for
motorcycles

P Pay & Display Bays:
Motorcyclists have to pay

Bus Lanes:
Not permitted to motorcycles

P Local Parking Contact:
Tel: 01934 634 706

Page/Ref	Town Address	Dealer name	Telephone no. Dealer website	Facilities	Dealer type
38 B4	Barnstaple Mill Road, Barnstaple, EX31 1JQ	Alex Buckingham Motorcycles	01271 329442 www.alexbuckinghammotorcycles.com	C	
38 B4	Barnstaple Units K1-K4 Mill Road Trad Est, Mill Road, Barnstaple, EX31 1JQ	Hedgehog Motorcycles	01271 326040 www.hedgehogmotorcycles.co.uk	C	
38 B4	Barnstaple Unit 6 Two River Ind Est, Braunton Road, Barnstaple, EX31 1JY	Irelands Motorcycles	01271 374243 www.irelandsmotorcycles.com	C	
41 G1	Bath 16-18 Lyndhurst Road, Oldfield Park, Bath, BA2 3JH	Barton Motor of Bath	01225 427906 www.kawasakibreakers.co.uk		
41 G1	Bath 42 Third Avenue, Oldfield Park, Bath, BA2 3NZ	Bishop's of Bath Motorcycles	01225 421805 www.motorcyclessouthwest.co.uk		
41 G1	Bath 11 Green Park Mews, Midland Bridge, Bath, BA1 1JD	D & H Motorcycles	01225 331318 www.dandhmotorcycles.com		
36 B3	Bournemouth 179 Ashley Road, Boscombe, Bournemouth, BH1 4NL	Barclay Motorcycle Services	01202 394367 www.motorcyclesbournemouth.co.uk		
36 B3	Bournemouth 107 Southwick Road, Bournemouth, BH6 5PS	Battistinis	01202 437400 www.battistinis.co.uk	C	
36 B3	Bournemouth Southbourne Road, Bournemouth, BH6 5AQ	Bikerloans	0870 2461850 www.bikerloans.co.uk		
36 A3	Bournemouth 1002-1006, Wimborne Road, Moordown, Bournemouth, BH9 2DE	Bournemouth Kawasaki Ltd	01202 635140 www.bournemouth-kawasaki.co.uk		
36 B3	Bournemouth Palmerston Road, Bournemouth, BH1 4HW	Bournespeed Scooters	01202 304661 www.bournespeed.co.uk	A R	
36 A3	Bournemouth 324-326, Charminster Road, Bournemouth, BH8 9RT	Crescent Motorcycles	01202 512923 www.crescent-suzuki.com	C	
36 B3	Bournemouth Ashley Road, Bournemouth, BH1 4NL *The South's Best Workshop.* *Dorset's major MOT Testing Centre.* *Full DYNO Rolling Road Facilities.* *Full Service @ £160.00 inc VAT and Parts!!!!* *Specialists in all Japanese and Italian Sports Bikes.*	Dynomite	01202 301201 www.dynomite.co.uk	A C R	
36 A3	Bournemouth Wimbourne Road, Mooredown, Bournemouth, BH9 2EG	Hein Gericke (UK) Ltd	01202 527200 www.hein-gericke.com	C	
36 A3	Bournemouth Unit 17-18 West Howe Ind Est, Elliot Road, Bournemouth, BH11 8JU	Motorcycle Tradeins	01202 576648 www.motorcycletradeins.com		
36 A3	Bournemouth Columbia Road, Bournemouth, BH10 4DZ	Mr Moped	01202 466268 www.mrmoped.co.uk	A C R	
36 B3	Bournemouth 57-61 Ashley Road, Boscombe, Bournemouth, BH1 4LG	Phils Motorcycle Mall	01202 302749 www.philsmall.co.uk	C	
36 A3	Bournemouth Charminster Avenue, Bournemouth, BH9 1RY	Ramoto	01202 523999 www.ramoto.com		
36 A3	Bournemouth Seabourne Road, Southbourne, Bournemouth, BH14 9DL	Roger Barrett Motorcycles	01202 718990 www.motoxtreme.co.uk	A C R	
36 A3	Bournemouth Elliott Road, West Howe Industrial Estate, Bournemouth, BH11 8JU	Spanners Motorcycle Services	01202 582000 www.spannersmotorcycles.co.uk	A C R	
36 A3	Bournemouth Wimborne Road, Bournemouth, BH9 2BN	Velocity Scooters	01202 512125 www.velocity-scooters.com	A R	
40 C4	Bridgwater East Quay Park, East Quay, Bridgwater, TA6 4DB	AFB Motorcycles	01278 444303 www.afbmotorcycles.co.uk	A C R	
40 C4	Bridgwater Eastover, Bridgwater, TA6 5AW	Generation Motorcycles	01278 431038	A C R	

Page/Ref	Town / Address	Dealer name	Telephone no. / Dealer website	Facilities	Dealer type
40 B4	Bridgwater Berrydale Avenue, Bridgwater, TA6 3QU	Mini Motos & Dirt Bikes	01278 431038		
40 B4	Bridgwater Saint Mary Street, Bridgwater, TA6 3LY	Pat Watts	01278 447165	A R	
40 C4	Bridgwater Riders House Wylds Road, Bridgwater, TA6 4BH	Riders Bridgwater Ltd	01278 457652 www.ridersofbristol.co.uk	A C R	
40 C4	Bridgwater Riverside Business Park, Bridgwater, TA6 4BH	V & J Honda	01278 410110 www.vandjsuperbikes.com	A C R	
44 D5	Bristol Bath Road, Bristol, BS4 3EZ	Aplin's	0117 9777376	A	
44 D5	Bristol Bath Road, Bristol, BS4 3EU	Bath Road Motorcycles	0117 9724444 www.bathroadmotorcycles.co.uk	A C	
44 D5	Bristol Castle House, Ducie Road, Bristol, BS5 0AJ	Bike Direct	01179 559553 www.bikedirectbristol.co.uk		
44 D5	Bristol Bristol St, Bristol, BS2 0PX	Bristol Kawasaki	0117 9772272	A	
44 D5	Bristol Bath Road, Arnos Vale, Bristol, BS4 3EW	Bristol Motorad	0117 9711447 www.nxgn-ltd.com		
44 D5	Bristol 15 Cleeve Wood Road, Downend, Bristol, BS16 2SF	Downend Scooters	01179 567899 www.downendbikesandscooters.co.uk	C	
44 C4	Bristol MMT Centre, Severn Bridge, Bristol, BS35 4BL	E-Bike	0870 7518138		
44 C5	Bristol North St, Bristol, BS3 1HJ	Fanatic Scooters	0117 9028656 www.fanaticscooters.co.uk		
44 C5	Bristol 2 Bath Road, Pylle Hill, Bristol, BS4 3DR	Fowlers Motorcycles	01179 770466 www.fowlers.co.uk	C	
44 C5	Bristol 59-61 Pembroke Road, Shirehampton, Bristol, BS11 9SA	George White Superbike Centre	0117 9823042 www.georgewhite.co.uk		
44 D5	Bristol Two Mile Hill Road, Bristol, BS15 1AS	Get Smart Scooters	0117 9601212 www.georgewhite.co.uk	A R	
44 C5	Bristol West St, Bristol, BS2 0BX	H.R.S Motorcycles	0117 9405555	A	
44 C5	Bristol Croft House Stokes Croft, Stockers Croft Road, Bristol, BS1 3TB	Hein Gericke (UK) Ltd	0117 9244942 www.hein-gericke.com	C	
41 F1	Bristol Unit 3 Unity Court, Broadmead Lane, Kenysham, Bristol, BS31 1ST	JHS Racing	01179 868844 www.jhsracing.co.uk		
44 C5	Bristol Kellaway Avenue, Bristol, BS6 7YQ	Kellaway Motorcycles	0117 9245491	A C R	
44 D5	Bristol 137 Church Road, Redfield, Bristol, BS5 9LA	M.R. Motorcycles	01179 552813 www.mrmotorcycles.com		
44 D5	Bristol Fishponds Road, Bristol, BS5 6PR	Matt's (Bristol) Ltd	0117 9517609 www.mattsmotorcyclesbristol.co.uk	R	
44 C5	Bristol Ashley Road, Bristol, BS6 5PA	Overbury's Specialist Cycles	0117 9557924	A C R	
44 D5	Bristol Stockwood Road, Bristol, BS4 5LR	Riders of Bristol	0117 9588777 www.ridersofbristol.co.uk	A C R	
45 D5	Bristol New Cheltenham Road, Bristol, BS15 1UL	Scoot 'N' Commute 2000	0117 9672000 www.scootandcommute.co.uk	A C R	

Page/Ref	Town Address	Dealer name	Telephone no. Dealer website	Facilities	Dealer type
44 D5	**Bristol** Strachan & Henshaw Building, Foundry Lane, Bristol, BS5 7UZ	**Scooter Tech**	0117 9652437	A R	⚫
44 D5	**Bristol** 2a Downend Road, Fishponds, Bristol, BS16 5AP	**Speedwell Motorcycles Ltd**	01179 654573 www.speedwellmotorcycles.com	C	⚫
44 D5	**Bristol** Eldon Wall Trading Estate, Bristol, BS4 3QQ	**Superbyke Ltd**	0117 3005746 www.superbyke.co.uk	A C R	⚫
44 D5	**Bristol** Lodge Causeway, Bristol, BS16 3JY	**T.N.R. Motorcycles**	0117 9657072 www.bristolkawasaki.co.uk		⚫
45 D4	**Bristol** Backfield Farm, Wotton Road, Iron Acton, Bristol, BS37 9XD	**The Bike Hut**	01454 228593 www.bikehutbristol.co.uk		⚫
44 C5	**Bristol** Bristol Vale Trading Estate, Hartcliffe Way, Bristol, BS3 5RJ	**The Bike Shop**	0117 9667988	A C R	⚫
44 C5	**Bristol** 208 West Street, Bedminster, Bristol, BS3 3NB	**Victor Motorcycles**	01179 665678		⚫
44 D5	**Bristol** 200 Church Road, Redfield, Bristol, BS5 8AD	**Wheel Torque**	01175 411014 www.wheeltorque.com	C	⚫
40 C3	**Burnham-On-Sea** Westmans Ind Est, Burnham-On-Sea, TA8 1EY	**Dog Motorcycles**	01278 785013 www.dogmotorcycles.co.uk	A C R	⚫
45 G5	**Calne** Wood St, Calne, SN11 0DA	**P. R. Taylor & Sons**	01249 812259		⚫
24 D2	**Cambourne** 14 Pendarves Street, Tucking Mill, Cambourne, TR14 8AF	**Anton Parris**	01209 719767 www.antonparris.co.uk		⚫
34 A2	**Chard** Millfield, Chard, TA20 2BB	**Lewis Motors**	01460 63095 www.lewis-motors.co.uk		⚫
34 A2	**Chard** Church Street Garage Church St, Chard, TA20 4JD	**Rhino Trikes**	01460 30170 www.rhino-trikes.co.uk	A	⚫
46 A5	**Chippenham** Webbs Court, Chippenham, SN15 4TR	**Moto-Vation**	01249 891263 www.moto-vation.net		⚫
45 E5	**Chippenham** Bell Square, Tormarton Road, Chippenham, SN14 8NN	**Motoxtreme**	01225 892227 www.motoxtreme.co.uk	C	⚫
36 B3	**Christchurch** Purewell, Christchurch, BH23 1EJ	**Bikers Yard Ltd**	01202 496006 www.bikersyard.co.uk		⚫
36 B3	**Christchurch** Burley Road, Christchurch, BH23 8DF	**Euroteam Services**	01425 674240	R	⚫
36 B3	**Christchurch** The Grove, Christchurch, BH23 2HB	**Malmesbury Motorcycles**	01202 477768 www.malmesburymotorcycles.co.uk		⚫
36 B3	**Christchurch** 143 Barrack Road, Christchurch, BH23 2AW	**Motorbiking Bournemouth**	01202 479125 www.motorbiking.co.uk		⚫
36 B3	**Christchurch** Barrack Road, Christchurch, BH23 2AR	**Powersport Motorcycles**	01202 485645	A R	⚫
36 B3	**Christchurch** Barrack Road, Christchurch, BH23 2AR	**Smart Riders**	01202 470566 www.smart-riders.co.uk	C	⚫
45 D1	**Cinderford** High St, Cinderford, GL14 2TB	**Haines & Co (Motorcycles) Ltd**	01594 822202 www.hainesmc.co.uk		⚫
46 A2	**Cirencester** Watermoor Road, Cirencester, GL7 1LD	**Hammond**	01285 652467 www.hammondmotorcycles.co.uk	A C R	⚫
44 B5	**Clevedon** Old St, Clevedon, BS21 6BW	**Clevedon Motorcycles**	01275 340909 www.clevedon-motorcycles.co.uk	A C R	⚫

Page/Ref		Town / Address	Dealer name	Telephone no. / Dealer website	Facilities	Dealer type
32	C3	**Crediton** Charlotte Street, Crediton, EX17 3BG	**Treen Motors**	01363 772283	A C R	
32	D4	**Exeter** Hennock Road North, Exeter, EX2 8NJ	**Albion Motorcycles Ltd**	01392 260340 www.albion.gb.com	A R	
32	D4	**Exeter** Isca Road, Exeter, EX2 8BH	**Bike Worx**	01392 272722 www.bikeworx.chinesemotorcycledealers.co.uk	A C R	
32	D4	**Exeter** Alphinbrook Road, Marsh Barton Trading Estate, Exeter, EX2 8RG	**Bridge Motorcycles Ltd**	01392 260200	A C R	
33	D4	**Exeter** Vennybridge, Exeter, EX4 8JJ	**CMS Motorcycle Parts**	01392 202666	A C	
33	E4	**Exeter** Unit 2, Aylesbeare Common Business Park, Exeter, EX5 2DG	**Chinese Motorcycle Dealers**	01395 233128 www.chinesemotorcycledealers.co.uk		
32	D4	**Exeter** Water Lane, Exeter, EX2 8BZ	**Chopper Haven**	01392 204115 www.chopperhaven.co.uk	A C R	
32	D4	**Exeter** Alphinbrook Road, Exeter, EX2 8RG	**Dynomap Motorcycles**	01392 495001 www.italian-motorcycle.co.uk	A R	
32	D4	**Exeter** 8 Alphinbrook Road, Exeter, EX2 8RG	**Greenlane Motorcycles**	01392 252111 www.greenlane-motorcycles.co.uk	C	
32	C4	**Exeter** Lower Trelake Business Park, Tedburn Road, Exeter, EX4 2HF	**HEL Performance Products**	01392 811601 www.h-e-l.co.uk	C	
32	D5	**Exeter** Leigham Business Units, Exeter, EX2 8HY	**MBT Customs Ltd**	01392 825687 www.mbtcustoms.co.uk	A C R	
32	D4	**Exeter** Hadrian Drive, Exeter, EX4 1SR	**Scoot N Commute**	01392 204432 www.scootandcommute.co.uk	A C	
32	D4	**Exeter** king Edward Street, Exeter, EX4 4NY	**Speed Superbike Centre**	01392 211246 www.speedthrills.co.uk		
32	D4	**Exeter** Colleton Crescent, Exeter, EX2 4DG	**Thompson Jenner**	01392 258553 www.thompson-jenner.co.uk		
45	F1	**Gloucester** Priory Road, Gloucester, GL1 2RQ	**Abingdon Honda**	01452 412000 www.abingdonhonda.co.uk	A R	
45	F1	**Gloucester** 12 Spinnaker Road, Hempsted, Gloucester, GL2 5FD	**Bransons Motorcycles**	01452 313131 www.bransonsmotorcycles.co.uk	C	
45	F1	**Gloucester** 261 Bristol Road, Gloucester, GL2 5DB	**Frasers of Gloucester Ltd**	01452 525128 www.frasersofgloucester.co.uk	C	
45	F1	**Gloucester** 3 Bramble Lawn, Abbeydale, Gloucester, GL4 5YF	**JJ Trade Sales**	01452 725009 www.jjtradesales.co.uk		
45	F1	**Gloucester** 64 High Street, Gloucester, GL1 4SR	**Tredworth Motorcycles**	01452 301513 www.tredmc.co.uk	C	
40	C3	**Highbridge** Main Road, Highbridge, TA9 3QS	**Stuart Motorcycles**	01278 793252		
42	B1	**Melksham** Watsons Court, Melksham, SN12 6JX	**Bob Missen**	01225 702325		
36	C3	**New Milton** Old Milton Road, New Milton, BH25 6DX	**Bursey Engineering**	01425 618739	A	
29	E1	**Newton Abbot** Queen St, Newton Abbot, TQ12 2BG	**Torbay Motorcycles**	01626 352527 www.torbaymc.eclipse.co.uk	A C R	

We are a friendly local dealership with over 40 years experience as Honda main dealer, we aim to cater for all customers providing the care and attention that has kept us in business all these years and keeps our customers coming back for more. We offer new and used bike sales with the backup you would expect from a Honda main dealer along side parts, clothing, accessories and full workshop facilities.

Page/Ref	Town Address	Dealer name	Telephone no. Dealer website	Facilities	Dealer type
33 E4	**Ottery St. Mary** Mill St, Ottery St. Mary, EX11 1AJ	**Browns Motorcycles**	*01404 813853* www.brownsmotorcycles.co.uk	*A C R*	◕
29 E2	**Paignton** Torquay Road, Paignton, TQ3 2SE	**GT Motorcycles Torbay**	*01803 559949* www.gtmotorcycles.com	*A C R*	◕
24 B3	**Penzance** Albert Street, Penzance, TR18 2LR	**Rieju UK Ltd**	*01736 351183* www.rieju.co.uk		◕
28 A3	**Plymouth** Crownhill Fort, Crownhill, Plymouth, PL5 2LX	**Classic Project Bikes**	*01822 610129*		◕
28 A3	**Plymouth** 214 Exeter Street, Plymouth, PL4 0NH	**Cool Moto**	*01752 665200* www.coolmoto.co.uk	*C*	◕
28 A3	**Plymouth** 99 Mutley Plain, Plymouth, PL4 6JJ	**Damerells Motorcycles**	*01752 667806* www.damerells.co.uk	*C*	◕
28 A3	**Plymouth** 55 Union Street, Plymouth, PL1 3LU	**E & E Motorcycles**	*01752 665141*		◕
28 A3	**Plymouth** 152-158, Albert Road, Devonport, Plymouth, PL2 1AQ *GT Motorcycles Torbay, 77-79 Torquay Road, Paignton, Devon, TQ3 2SE Tel: 01803 559949 is part of a three location dealership: Plymouth, Torbay and St Austell. Between us we cover Yamaha, Suzuki, Kawasaki, Triumph, Aprilia and all the main scooter manufacturers. Large enough to rely on, small enough to care.*	**GT Motorcycles**	*01752 559063* www.gtmotorcycles.com	*C*	◕
28 A3	**Plymouth** Alice St Garage, 1 Alice St, Plymouth, PL1 1AS	**Jerry's Motorcycle Refinishers**	*01752 229227* www.motorcycle-repairs.co.uk	*A R*	◕
28 A3	**Plymouth** Beaumont Road, Plymouth, PL4 9BP	**Kenhard Motorcycles**	*01752 266275*	*A R*	◕
28 B3	**Plymouth** Market Road, Plymouth, PL7 1QW	**M S C Motorcycles**	*01752 346000*		◕
28 A3	**Plymouth** Union St, Plymouth, PL1 3HL	**Right Price Motorcycles Ltd**	*01752 252685*	*A C R*	◕
28 A3	**Plymouth** Carlton Terrace Eldad Hill, Plymouth, PL1 5EA	**Western Spares**	*01752 669925*	*A C R*	◕
36 A3	**Poole** Bournemouth Road, Poole, BH14 9HU	**G R's Sports Bikes**	*01202 737876* www.grssportsbikes.com	*A R*	◕
36 A3	**Poole** 138 Stanely Green Road, Poole, BH15 3AH	**Poole Motorcycles**	*01202 670023* www.poole-motorcycles.co.uk	*C*	◕
36 A3	**Poole** Ashley Road, Parkstone, Poole, BH14 9DL	**Roger Barrett Scooters**	*01202 426244*	*A C R*	◕
36 A3	**Poole** Ashley Road, Poole, BH14 9DL	**Select Motorcycles**	*01202 744557*		◕
41 F2	**Radstock** Old Pit Garage Coombend, Radstock, BA3 3AT	**Parsons Motorcycles (Radstock)**	*01761 433522*	*A C R*	◕
36 B2	**Ringwood** Hightown Industrial Estate, Crow Arch Lane, Ringwood, BH24 1ND	**In Chains Motorcycles**	*01425 474800*	*C*	◕
43 D3	**Salisbury** The Centre, Amesbury, Salisbury, SP4 7DR	**A. K. Motor Spares**	*01980 622106* www.akmotorspares.org.uk		◕
43 D5	**Salisbury** The Headlands, Downton, Salisbury, SP5 3HH	**Burnout Bikes**	*01725 510288* www.burnoutbikes.co.uk	*C*	◕
42 D4	**Salisbury** Churchfields Industrial Estate, Brunel Road, Salisbury, SP2 7PU	**Hayball Motorcycles Ltd**	*01722 322796* www.hayball.co.uk		◕
43 D3	**Near Salisbury** Bulford Road, Durrington, Near Salisbury, SP4 8DL	**Rangers**	*01980 653434* www.peugeotmilitarysales.co.uk		◕

Page/Ref	Town Address	Dealer name	Telephone no. Dealer website	Facilities	Dealer type
28 C3	South Brent Blacksmith Lane, South Brent, TQ10 9HX	South Devon Motorcycle Services	01364 73920 www.the-internet-pages.co.uk/england/exet/cycles1/sdm.htm	A R	
45 F2	Stroud London Road, Stroud, GL5 2DA	B. V. M. Moto	01453 762167 www.bvm-moto.co.uk	A C R	
45 F2	Stroud Wallbridge Mill, 10 Wallbridge Ind Est, Stroud, GL5 3JU	Bar Ash Motorcycles	01453 758963	A R	
45 F2	Stroud Bath Road, Stroud, GL5 3TA	Roadrunner Motorcycles	01453 755034	A C R	
46 B4	Swindon Rodbourne Road, Swindon, SN2 2AA	Artdeans.co.uk	01793 574800 www.artdeans.co.uk		
46 A4	Swindon Edmonds Garage, Coped Hall, Swindon, SN4 8ES	B J C Motorcycles	01793 849661 www.bjctrailtours.co.uk		
46 A4	Swindon Oak Farm, Swindon, SN5 0AG	Bill Little Classic Motorcycles	01666 860577		
46 B4	Swindon Manchester Road, Swindon, SN1 2AJ	Budget Bikes	01793 422236 www.budgetbikesmotorcycles.co.uk		
46 A3	Swindon Bath Road, Swindon, SN6 6EL	Elliott Motorcycles	01793 751752 www.elliottmc.co.uk	A C R	
46 B4	Swindon 1 Manchester Road, Swindon, SN1 2AB	George White Superbike Centre	01793 716716 www.georgewhite.co.uk		
46 B4	Swindon Kingsdown Ind Est, Stratton St. Margaret, Swindon, SN25 6PD	Steve Lynham	01793 820630		
46 B4	Swindon Kingsdown Ind Est, Stratton St. Margaret, Swindon, SN25 6PD	Swindon Classic Bikes	01793 829560 www.swindonclassicbikes.com	A C R	
40 C4	Taunton Church Street, Bridge Water, Taunton, TA6 5AS	Anderson & Wall	01278 423089 www.anderson-wall.co.uk	A C R	
33 G1	Taunton 57 Station Road, Taunton, TA1 1NZ	Anderson & Wall	01823 323353 www.anderson-wall.co.uk	C	
33 G1	Taunton Wellington Road, Taunton, TA1 5LA	Atkins of Taunton	01823 254555 www.atkinsoftaunton.co.uk	A R	
33 G1	Taunton Riverside Works, Bridgewater Road, Bathpool, Taunton, TA1 2DX	Bitzabikes	01823 251973		
33 G1	Taunton Pooles Garage, Whitehall, Taunton, TA1 1PG	G V Bikes	01823 276012 www.gvbikes.co.uk		
33 G1	Taunton 45 Wood Street, Taunton, TA1 1UW	Graham's Motorcycles	01823 331397 www.grahamsmotorcycles.com	C	
33 G1	Taunton 9 Silver Street, Taunton, TA1 3DH	Superbikes Southwest Ltd	01823 325222 www.super-bikes.biz	C	
33 G1	Taunton 43-45 East Reach, Taunton, TA1 3ES	V & J Suzuki	01823 272378 www.vandjsuperbikes.co.uk	C	
33 G1	Taunton 47 East Reach, Taunton, TA1 3EX	V & J Yamaha	01823 323277 www.vandjsuperbikes.co.uk	C	
29 F2	Torquay Broomhill Way, Torquay, TQ2 7QL	PGH Motorcycles	01803 676764 www.pghmotorcycles.com	C	
29 F2	Torquay Union St, Torquay, TQ2 5QU	Torre Motorcycles	01803 294184	A C R	
29 E2	Totnes Warland Garage 15a Warland, Totnes, TQ9 5EL	B. R. Trott	01803 862493 www.brtrott.co.uk	C R	
29 D2	Totnes Cedar Units, Totnes, TQ9 6JY	Roger Neale	01803 866064		

Page/Ref		Town Address	Dealer name	Telephone no. Dealer website	Facilities	Dealer type
42	A2	**Trowbridge** Bradley Road, Trowbridge, BA14 0QX	**Phoenix Motorcycles**	*01225 775171* www.phoenixmc.co.uk	A C R	
36	B2	**Verwood** Black Moor Road, Verwood, BH31 6AX	**Crescent Racing Ltd**	*01202 820170* www.crescent-suzuki.com	A C R	
35	G4	**Wareham** Johns Road, Wareham, BH20 4BG	**Motosport Motorcycle Centre**	*01929 555003*		
42	A3	**Warminster** Woodcock Ind Est, Warminster, BA12 9DX	**Roy Vincent**	*01985 219195*	A	
35	D5	**Weymouth** Unit 1a Granby Industrial Estate, Weymouth, DT4 9TY	**Fat Armadillo**	*01305 839988* www.fatarmadillo.com		
36	A2	**Wimborne** Woolbridge Industrial Estate, Victory Close, Wimborne, BH21 6SX	**Conquest**	*01202 820009*	A R	
36	A2	**Wimborne** Thorne Way, Wimborne, BH21 6SB	**GCS Motorcycle Services**	*01202 826045*	A R	
36	A2	**Wimborne** Old Barn Farm Road, Wimborne, BH21 6SP	**Moto Corsa**	*01202 822511* www.motocorsa.com	A R	
36	A2	**Wimborne** Woolbridge Industrial Estate, Wimborne, BH21 6Sp	**Renntec**	*01202 826722* www.renntec.co.uk		
36	A2	**Wimborne** Old Barn Farm Road, Wimborne, BH21 6SP	**Three Cross Motorcycles Ltd**	*01202 824531* www.3xmotorcycles.net	A C R	
34	C1	**Yeovil** Unit 13b The Old Sawmills, Halves Lane, Yeovil, BA22 9JJ	**Black Dragon Motorcycles**	*01935 864167* www.blackdragonmotorcycles.co.uk	C	
34	C1	**Yeovil** 7 Pen Mill Trading Estate, Oxford Road, Yeovil, BA21 5HR	**Bransons Motorcycles**	*01935 474998* www.bransonsmotorcycles.co.uk	C	
34	C1	**Yeovil** 26 Pen Mill Trading Estate, Oxford Road, Yeovil, BA21 5HR	**Riders Yeovil Ltd**	*01935 421681* www.ridersmotorcycles.co.uk		
34	C1	**Yeovil** Main Street, Mudford, Yeovil, BA21 5TE	**V & J Suzuki**	*01935 850505* www.vandjsuperbikes.co.uk	C	

*Huge selection of new and used motorcycles, incl. Suzuki,
Honda and Yamaha from any of our four exclusive dealerships
at V and J Superbikes. Based at Taunton, Bridgwater and Yeovil
in Somerset, our fully factory trained staff are committed to
offering a great range of motorcycles and scooters as well as
great service to ensure that you get not only the right bike for you
but the best possible deal available.*

Parking for Bikes.com
www.thePIEguide.com

"The rider's website for maps and local information"

The essential one-stop online guide for bike riders. It provides
all the vital information required before setting out, from route
planning to finding petrol stations and parking bays.

✓ Postcode search tool
✓ Free & discounted car park locations
✓ Maps detailing free residential pay & display bays

Page/Ref		Town Address	Name	Telephone no. Website	Facilities	Accommodation type
28	D1	**Ashburton** Tavistock Road, Near Ashburton, TQ13 7NS	Holne Chase Hotel	01364 631471 www.holne-chase.co.uk	P L W	HOTEL
46	A5	**Near Avebury** The New Inn, Monkton, Near Avebury, SN4 9NW	The New Inn	01672 539240 www.thenewinn.net	P L W D	B&B
41	F1	**Bath** Clifton Hill, Bath, BS39 5QL	The Hunts Rest Inn	01761 452303 www.huntsrest.co.uk	P L W	HOTEL
41	G2	**Bath** Combe Hay, Bath, BA2 7EG	Wheatsheaf Inn	01225 833504 www.wheatsheafcombehay.com	P L	HOTEL
35	F3	**Bere Regis** West Street, Bere Regis, BH20 7HQ	The Royal Oak	01929 471203 www.theroyaloakhotel.co.uk	P V L	HOTEL
31	F1	**Bideford** Atlantic Way, Westward Ho!, Bideford, EX39 1JG	Broomhayes Manor	01237 477716	P	B&B
31	E1	**Bideford** Acre Lane, Horns Cross, Bideford, EX39 5DH	Maecroft	0123 745 1786	G P W	B&B
31	F1	**Bideford** Monkleigh, Bideford, EX39 5JR	Monkleigh House	01805 625453 www.monkleighhouse.co.uk	P V	B&B
31	F1	**Bideford** Old Barnstable Road, Eastleigh, Bideford, EX39 4PA	The Pines At Eastleigh	01271 860561 www.4hotels.co.uk	P	HOTEL
35	G2	**Blandford** Salisbury Road, Pimperne, Blandford, DT11 8UQ	The Anvil Inn	01258 453431 www.anvilinn.co.uk	P L	HOTEL
36	B3	**Bournemouth** Knole Road, Bournemouth, BH1 4DH *Abbey Court may be small but big on customer service, clean & comfy, good food, home from home. We have safe secure parking under camera, lock & key. We are just a short walk from gardens, beaches, towns etc. An excellent location for touring the South West & areas.*	Abbey Court Hotel	01202 300883 www.abbeycourtbournemouth.co.uk	P	HOTEL
36	B3	**Bournemouth** Knole Road, Bournemouth, BH1 4DQ	The Park Hotel	01202 467903 www.aparkhotel.co.uk	G P L	HOTEL
42	B1	**Bromham** Chittoe Heath, Bromham, SN15 2EH	Wayside	01380 850695 www.waysideofwiltshire.co.uk	P	B&B
28	D2	**Buckfastleigh** Buckfast Road, Buckfast, Buckfastleigh, TQ11 0EA	The Abbey Inn	01364 642343 www.abbey-inn.co.uk	P V L	B&B
30	D2	**Bude** Sandymouth Bay, Bude, EX23 9HW	Houndapitt Farm Cottages	0128 835 5455 www.houndapitt.co.uk	P W	SELF CATERING
30	C4	**Bude** Crackington Haven, Bude, EX23 0JG	The Coombe Barton Inn	01840 230345 www.coombebarton.co.uk	P L	HOTEL
30	D3	**Bude** Widemouth Bay, Bude, EX23 0DE	The Widemouth Manor Hotel	01288 361263 www.widemouthmanor.co.uk	P V L	HOTEL
30	D2	**Near Bude** Morwenstow, Near Bude, EX23 9SJ	Willow Tree Cottage	01288 331100 www.willowtreecottage.co.uk	P D	B&B
46	B5	**Chiseldun** Draycott Road, Chiseldun, SN4 0LS	Courtleigh House B&B	01793 740246	G P W	B&B
46	B2	**Cirencester** The High Street, Meysey Hampton, Cirencester, GL7 5JP	Angells House	01285 851804 angellshouse.co.uk	G P W	B&B
46	A2	**Cirencester** Coxwell Street, Cirencester, GL7 2BQ	Old Court	01285 653164 www.old-court.co.uk	P W	B&B
46	B3	**Cirencester** High Street, Meysey Hampton, Cirencester, GL7 5JT	The Masons Arms	01285 850164	P V L W D	HOTEL
46	A3	**Cirencester** Ewen, Cirencester, GL7 6BY	The Wild Duck	01285 770310 www.thewildduckinn.co.uk	P V L W D	HOTEL
44	C1	**Coleford** Monmouth Road, Edge End, Coleford, GL16 7HB	Cor-Unum	01594 837960 www.cor-unum.co.uk	G W	SELF CATERING
28	A3	**Cremyll** Cremyll Quay, Cremyll, Near Plymouth, PL10 1HX	Edgecombe Arms	01752 822294	V L	B&B
42	C1	**Devizes** Downlands Road, Devizes, SN10 5EF	Asta B&B	01380 722546 www.ukbed.com	P W D	B&B
42	B2	**Devizes** Coxhill Lane, Potterne, Devizes, SN10 5PH	Blounts Court Farm	01380 727180 www.blountscourtfarm.co.uk	P	B&B

Page/Ref	Town Address	Name	Telephone no. Website	Facilities	Accommodation type
42 B2	Devizes Littleton Panell, Devizes, SN10 4ES	Littleton Lodge	01380 813131 www.littletonlodge.co.uk	P	B&B
42 B2	Near Devizes Lower Rd, Erlestoke, Near Devizes, SN10 5UE	Longwater	01380 830095 	P	B&B
42 C1	Devizes Roundway, Devizes, SN10 2HZ	Roundway Farm House B&B	01380 723113 roundwayfarm.com	G P W D	B&B
42 C1	Devizes Market Place, Devizes, SN10 1JQ	The Black Swan Hotel	01380 723259 www.blackswanhotel.fsnet.co.uk	P V L W D	HOTEL
42 C2	Devizes High Street, Devizes, SN10 4AG	The Green Dragon	01380 813235 www.greendragonlavington.co.uk	G P L D	HOTEL
35 E2	Dorchester Piddletrenthide, Dorchester, DT2 7QX	Poachers Inn	01300 348358 www.thepoachersinn.co.uk	P L W	HOTEL

The Poachers Inn, renowned in Dorset for its sumptuous 21-room accommodation, 17th Century restaurant and beautiful riverside garden. We are passionate about using the finest local ingredients with meat, fish, game, bread and cheese from local suppliers. Open all day with food served from noon till 9.30. Additional parking at rear.

Page/Ref	Town Address	Name	Telephone no. Website	Facilities	Accommodation type
35 E2	Near Dorchester Ansty, Near Dorchester, DT2 7PN	The Fox Inn	01258 880328	P L	B&B
39 F4	Near Dunster Luxborough, Near Dunster, TA23 0SH	The Royal Oak Inn	01984 640319 www.theroyaloakinnluxborough.co.uk	P L D	HOTEL
33 D5	Exeter Fore Street, Topsham, Exeter, EX3 0HU	Galley Fish Restaurant & Cabins	01392 876078 www.galleyrestaurant.co.uk	P L D	SELF CATERING
33 D4	Exeter Oil Mill Lane, Clyst St. Mary, Exeter, EX5 1AG	Kiddicott Farm	01392 879032 www.kiddicottfarm.com	P	B&B
32 D4	Exeter Howell Road, Exeter, EX4 4LG	Park View Hotel	01392 271772 www.parkviewexeter.co.uk	P	B&B
32 D4	Exeter Backall Road, Exeter, EX4 4HD	Raffles Hotel	01392 270200 www.raffles-exeter.co.uk	P L D	B&B
32 D4	Exeter East Wonford Hill, Exeter, EX1 3TF	Road Lodge	01392 438200 www.roadlodge.co.uk	P W D	B&B
39 E4	Exford Chapel Street, Exford, TA24 7PY	Exmoor Lodge Guest House	01643 831694	L W D	B&B
25 F3	Falmouth Melvill Road, Falmouth, TR11 4AR	Mermaid Lodge	01326 313489 www.mermaidlodge.com	P W D	B&B
25 F3	Falmouth Gyllyngvase Hill, Gyllyngvase Beach, Falmouth, TR11 4DN	Rathgowry Hotel	01326 313482 www.rathgowry.co.uk	P	HOTEL
41 E5	Ilchester Ilchester, BA22 8LD	Northhover Manor Hotel	01935 840447 www.northovermanor.com	P L W	HOTEL
38 B3	Ilfracombe Fore Street, Ilfracombe, EX34 9ED	Ablemarle & Harbour's End Holiday Aparts.	01271 862951 www.ilfracombe-holiday.co.uk	P W D	SELF CATERING
31 E5	Launceston Higher Bamham, Launceston, PL15 9LD	Bamham Farm Cottages	0156 677 2141 www.cottages-cornwall.co.uk	P W	SELF CATERING
27 F3	Looe Barbican Hill, Looe, PL13 1BQ	Haven House Bed & Breakfast	01503 264160 www.bedbreakfastlooe.co.uk	P	B&B
27 F3	Near Looe Jubilee Hill, Pelynt, Near Looe, PL13 2JZ	Jubilee Inn	01503 220312 www.information-britain.co.uk	P L	HOTEL
34 A3	Lyme Regis Hill Road, Lyme Regis, DT7 3PE	Manaton	0129 7445138 www.manaton.net	P	B&B
34 A3	Lyme Regis Broad Street, Lyme Regis, DT7 3QE	The Smuggler	01297 442795 www.lymeregis.com	P W	B&B
34 A3	Lyme Regis Off Lyme Road, Lyme Regis, DT7 3LP	Victoria Hotel	01297 444801 www.vichotel.co.uk	P L	HOTEL
38 D3	Lynmouth Harbourside, Lynmouth, EX35 6EG	The Rising Sun Hotel	01598 753223 www.specialplace.co.uk	L	HOTEL
38 D3	Lynton Lynbridge Road, Lynton, EX35 6BD	Valley House	01598 752285 www.valley-house.co.uk	P L	B&B
38 D3	Lynton Lynbridge Road, Lynton, EX35 6AX	Woodlands	01598 752324 www.woodlandsguesthouse.co.uk	P L W D	B&B

Page/Ref	Town / Address	Name	Telephone no. / Website	Facilities	Accommodation type
46 C5	**Marlborough** Marlborough Road, Ogbourne St George, Marlborough, SN8 1SQ	The Inn With The Well	01672 841445 www.theinnwiththewell.co.uk	P L	HOTEL
42 A4	**Mere** The Square, Mere, BA12 6DR	The George Inn	01747 860427 www.pubsulike.co.uk	P L W	HOTEL
39 D4	**Near Morehead** Simonsbath, Near Morehead, TA24 7SH	Simonsbath House	01643 831259 www.simonsbathhouse.co.uk	P L D	HOTEL

Overlooking the Barle Valley in the heart of Exmoor, Simonsbath is an ideal location to enjoy the wonderful biking offered by Somerset and North Devon. Simonsbath House offers a choice of accommodation with 10 ensuite bedrooms, three self-catering cottages for between 2-6 people and a fully catered dormitory sleeping up to 30 people. Special rates for groups. For further details contact 01643 831259 or Email: hotel@simonsbathhousehotel.co.uk

Page/Ref	Town / Address	Name	Telephone no. / Website	Facilities	Accommodation type
45 F3	**Nailsworth** Nailsworth, GL6 0AE	Egypt Mill Hotel	01453 833449 www.egyptmill.com	P L	HOTEL
45 F3	**Nailsworth** Rockness, Horsley, Nailsworth, GL6 0PJ	The Coach House	01453 832265 www.cotswoldholidaycottage.co.uk	P W D	SELF CATERING
26 B2	**Newquay** Tower Road, Newquay, TR7 1LY	Cotehele Lodge	01637 873421 www.cotehelelodge.co.uk	P V	B&B
26 B2	**Newquay** Mountwise, Newquay, TR7 2BS	Quies	01637 872924 www.quieshotelnewquay.co.uk	P W	HOTEL
26 B2	**Newquay** Alexandra Road, Porth Bay, Newquay, TR7 3NB	The Windward Hotel	01637 873185 www.windwardhotel.co.uk	P L D	HOTEL
39 E3	**North Minehead** High Street, Porlock, North Minehead, TA24 8PY	Rose Bank Guest House	0164 386 2728 www.rosebankguesthouse.co.uk	P W D	B&B
29 E3	**Paignton** Alta Vista Road, Roundham, Paignton, TQ4 6DB	Benbows Hotel	0180 355 8128 www.benbowshotel.co.uk	P L	HOTEL
29 E2	**Paignton** Colin Road, Paignton, TQ3 2NR	Innisfree Hotel	01803 550692 www.innisfreehotel.co.uk	P	B&B

Small family run guest house 100 metres from Preston Beach. Off road parking. TV, Tea / Coffee all rooms. En-suite available. Two Ground Floor rooms. Great base for exploring Coast and Moor. Hose available for bike cleaning.

Page/Ref	Town / Address	Name	Telephone no. / Website	Facilities	Accommodation type
29 E2	**Paignton** Adelphi Road, Paignton, TQ4 6AW	Tregarth Holiday Flats	0180 3558458 www.tregarthpaignton.co.uk	G P V W D	SELF CATERING
27 D3	**Par** Tywardreath Highway, Par, PL24 2RW	Palm Garden House	01726 816112 www.gbstay.co.uk	G P W	B&B
24 A3	**Pendeen** The Square, Pendeen, TR19 7DN	The North Inn	01736 788417 www.thenorthinnpendeen.co.uk	P L	B&B
24 A3	**Penzance** Pendeen, Penzance, TR19 7EP	Berry's Folly	01249 653377 www.berrys-folly.co.uk	P W	SELF CATERING
24 B4	**Penzance** Regent Terrace, Penzance, TR18 4DW	Camilla House Hotel	01736 363771 www.camillahouse.co.uk	P L	B&B
24 B4	**Penzance** Pridden Lane, St. Buryan, Penzance, TR19 6EA	Pridden	01736 810 801 www.—	P W D	SELF CATERING
24 A3	**Penzance** Market Square, St Just, Penzance, TR19 7HD	Wellington Hotel	01736 787319 www.wellington-hotel.co.uk	P L	HOTEL
42 D1	**Near Pewsey** Wilcot, Near Pewsey, SN9 5NN	The Golden Swan	01672 562289 www.goldenswan.co.uk	P L	B&B
42 D1	**Near Pewsey** Honey Street, Woodborough, Near Pewsey, SN9 5PS	Well Cottage	01672 851577 www.well-cottage.org.uk	P D	B&B
28 A3	**Plymouth** Pier Street, West Hoe, Plymouth, PL1 3BS	The Firs Guest House	01752 262870 www.uk-westcountry.co.uk	P	B&B
28 A3	**Plymouth** Citadel Road, The Hoe, Plymouth, PL1 2RN	Westwinds Guesthouse	01752 601777 www.westwindsplymouth.co.uk	P	B&B
25 E1	**St. Agnes** Trevaunance Cove, St. Agnes, TR5 0RT	Driftwood Spars Hotel	01872 552428 www.driftwoodspars.com	P L	HOTEL

Facilities: **G** = Garage parking **P** = Off Street parking **V** = CCTV Security **L** = Licensed premises **W** = Laundry **D** = Drying room

85

Page/Ref	Town / Address	Name	Telephone no. / Website	Facilities	Accommodation type
42 D4	Salisbury / Castle Road, Salisbury, SP1 3RH	The Edwardian Lodge Guest House	01722 413329 / www.edwardianlodge.co.uk	P	B&B
42 C4	Near Salisbury / Stoford, Near Salisbury, SP2 0PR	The Swan Inn	01722 790236 / www.theswanatstoford.co.uk	P L	HOTEL
43 D5	Near Salisbury / The Ridge, Woodfalls, Near Salisbury, SP5 2LN	The Woodfalls Inn	01725 513222 / www.woodfallsinn.co.uk	P L W	HOTEL
27 G2	Saltash / Stoketon Cross, Trematon, Saltash, PL12 4RZ	The Crooked Inn	01752 848177 / www.crooked-inn.co.uk	P L	HOTEL
24 A4	Sennen / Sennen Cove, Sennen, TR19 7DG	The Old Success Inn	01736 871232 / www.oldsuccess.com	P L W	HOTEL
41 F4	Near Shepton Mallet / Ditchet, Near Shepton Mallet, BA4 6RB	The Manor House Inn	01749 860276 / www.manorhouseinn.co.uk	P L W D	B&B
45 E2	Stonehouse / The Cross, Nympsfield, Stonehouse, GL10 3TU	Rose & Crown Inn	01453 860240 / www.roseandcrown-nympsfield.com	P L W	HOTEL
45 F4	Tetbury / Knockdown Rd, Tetbury, GL8 8QY	Holford Arms	01454 238669 /	P L	HOTEL
30 B5	Tintagel / Alantic Road, Tintagel, PL34 0DD	Wootons Country Hotel	0184 077 0170 / www.wootons.co.uk	P L	HOTEL
29 F2	Torquay / Morgan Avenue, Torquay, TQ2 5RS	Hillsborough Hotel	0180 329 3286 / www.hillsboroughhotel.co.uk	P D	HOTEL
29 F2	Torquay / Babbacombe Road, Torquay, TQ1 1HQ	The Palms Hotel	0180 3293970 / www.palmshoteltorquay.co.uk	P L	HOTEL
29 F2	Torquay / Scarborough Road, Torquay, TQ2 5UJ	The Westbrook	01803 292559 / www.westbrookhotel.net	P W	HOTEL
42 A1	Trowbridge / Marsh Road, Hilperton Marsh, Trowbridge, BA14 7PL	Ring O Bells Guest House	01225 754404 / www.ringobells.biz	P V W D	B&B

Formerly a pub, Ring O' Bells now offers non-smoking, comfortable en-suite rooms on the ground and first floors. Rooms have TV, tea/coffee facilities, radio/alarm, hairdryer & room-safes. Private Car Park, disabled access, WiFi internet via BT Openzone, friendly atmosphere. Child & Pet friendly. CCTV is in operation for your protection.

Page/Ref	Town / Address	Name	Telephone no. / Website	Facilities	Accommodation type
25 E1	Truro / Mithian Downs, Near St. Agnes, Truro, TR5 0QH	Valley View	0187 255 4475 / www.st-agnes-holiday-accommodation.co.uk	G P W D	SELF CATERING
32 A1	Umberleigh / Junction of A377 and B3227, Umberleigh, EX37 9DU	The Rising Sun Inn	01769 560447 / www.risingsuninn.com	P L	HOTEL
42 B3	Warminster / Corton, Warminster, BA12 0SZ	The Dove Inn	01985 850109 / www.thedove.co.uk	P L	HOTEL
25 E1	West Bay / Driftwood Apartments, Fort Foot Way, West Bay, TR8 5PQ	Driftwood Apartments	07766 522798 / www.driftwoodapartments.co.uk	P W	SELF CATERING
28 D1	Widecombe in the Moor / Widecombe in the Moor, Dartmoor, TQ13 7TT	Holwell Cottages	01364 631471 / www.holwelldartmoor.co.uk	P W D	SELF CATERING
46 B4	Wroughton / Swindon Road, Wroughton, SN4 9AG	Artis Cottage Guesthouse	01793 845424 / www.artis-cottage-guesthouse.co.uk	G P W	B&B

www.thePIEguide.com

Roads for Bikes.com

"The rider's website for maps and local information"

Get yourself listed online if you are a biker friendly:
accommodation, bar, café, restaurant, etc.

For a great site that only maps bike friendly establishments
and recommended roads.

Page/Ref		Town Address	Name	Telephone no. Bar website
41	G2	**Bath** Combe Hay, Bath, BA2 7EG	**Wheatsheaf Inn**	01225 833504 www.wheatsheafcombehay.com
36	A3	**Bournemouth** Old Christchurch Road, Bournemouth, BH1 1EW	**Daisy O'Briens**	01202 290002
36	A3	**Bournemouth** 27-29 West Hill Road, City Centre, Bournemouth, BH2 5PF	**Goat & Tricycle**	01202 314220
36	A3	**Bournemouth** Old Christchurch Road, Bournemouth, BH1 1JZ	**The Litten Tree**	01202 438001
36	A3	**Bournemouth** Old Christchurch Road, Bournemouth, BH2 6DT	**The Slug & Lettuce**	01202 317686 www.slugandlettuce.co.uk
28	A3	**Cremyll** Cremyll Quay, Cremyll, Near Plymouth, PL10 1HX	**Edgecombe Arms**	01752 822294
42	C2	**Devizes** High Street, Market Lavington, Devizes, SN10 4AG	**The Green Dragon**	01380 813235
32	D4	**Exeter** Sidwell Street, Exeter, EX4 6RH	**Amber Rooms**	01392 431420 www.amberrooms.co.uk
32	D4	**Exeter** Bonhay Road, Exeter, EX4 3AB	**Mill on the Exe**	01392 214464
32	D4	**Exeter** Red Cow Village, Exeter, EX4 4AX	**The Artful Dodger**	01392 274754
32	D4	**Exeter** Clifton Road, Exeter, EX1 2BR	**The Clifton Inn**	01392 273527
45	F1	**Gloucester** Southgate Street, Gloucester, GL1 1TS	**Café Rene**	01452 309340 www.caferene.co.uk
45	F1	**Gloucester** Bruton Way, Gloucester, GL1 1EP	**The Famous Pint Pot**	01452 416840
45	F1	**Gloucester** Shurdington Road, Gloucester, GL3 4PH	**Toby Carvery Brockworth**	01452 863441
27	F3	**Near Looe** Jubilee Hill, Pelynt, Near Looe, PL13 2JZ	**Jubilee Inn**	01503 220312 www.information-britain.co.uk
24	B3	**Penzance** Chapel Street, Penzance, TR18 4AF	**The Admiral Benbow**	01736 363448
24	B4	**Penzance** Alexandra Road, Penzance, TR18 4LS	**The Alexandra**	0176 365165
24	B4	**Penzance** Cornwall Terrace, Penzance, TR18 4HL	**The Bath Inn**	01736 331940
24	B4	**Penzance** Quay Street, Penzance, TR18 4BD	**The Dock Inn**	01736 362833
24	B3	**Penzance** Market Jew Street, Penzance, TR18 2LD	**The Star Inn**	01736 363241
28	A3	**Plymouth** 65 Union Street, Stonehouse, Plymouth, PL1 3LU	**The Clipper Inn**	01752 224221 www.theclipperinn.co.uk
28	B3	**Plymouth** Radford Park Road, Plymouth, PL9 9DN	**The Drakes Drum**	01752 402613
28	A3	**Plymouth** Anstis Street, Stonehouse, Plymouth, PL1 5JT	**The Duchy of Cornwall**	01752 294436 www.victoriainns.co.uk
28	A3	**Plymouth** Wolseley Road, Saltash Passage, Plymouth, PL5 1LA	**The Ferry House Inn**	01752 361063 www.railaletrail.com
28	A3	**Plymouth** Saltash Passage, Plymouth, PL5 1LB	**The Royal Albert Bridge Inn**	01752 361108
42	D5	**Salisbury** Catherine Street, Salisbury, SP1 2DH	**The Cloisters**	01722 338102
43	E4	**Salisbury** White Hill, Pitton, Salisbury, SP5 1DZ	**The Silver Plough**	01722 712266
27	G2	**Saltash** Stoketon Cross, Trematon, Saltash, PL12 4RZ	**The Crooked Inn**	01752 848177 www.crooked-inn.co.uk

Page/Ref		Town Address	Name	Telephone no. Bar website
45	E2	**Stonehouse**	**Rose & Crown Inn**	*01453 860240*
		The Cross, Nympsfield, Stonehouse, GL10 3TU		www.roseandcrown-nympsfield.com
46	C4	**Swindon**	**Brewers Arms**	*01793 790707*
		High Street, Wanborough, Swindon, SN4 0AE		www.brewers-arms.co.uk
46	B4	**Swindon**	**Casbah**	*01793 436020*
		John Street, Swindon, SN1 1RT		www.thecasbah.co.uk
46	B4	**Swindon**	**The Baker's Arms**	*01793 535199*
		Emlyn Square, Swindon, SN1 5BN		
46	B4	**Swindon**	**The Beehive**	*01793 523187*
		Prospect Hill, Swindon, SN1 3JS		
46	B4	**Swindon**	**The Victoria**	*01793 535713*
		Victoria Road, Swindon, SN1 3BD		www.thevicswindon.com
46	A4	**Near Swindon**	**The Curriers Arms**	*01793 854814*
		High Street, Wootton Bassett, Near Swindon, SN4 7AB		
46	B4	**Near Swindon**	**The Fox & Hounds**	*01793 812217*
		Markham Road, Wroughton, Near Swindon, SN4 9JT		
33	G1	**Taunton**	**Hankridge Arms**	*01823 444405*
		Hankridge Way, Riverside, Taunton, TA1 2LR		
33	G1	**Taunton**	**The Alma**	*01823 331627*
		Silver Street, Taunton, TA1 3DL		
33	G1	**Taunton**	**The Blackhorse Inn**	*01823 272151*
		Bridge Street, Taunton, TA1 1UD		
33	G1	**Taunton**	**The Racehorse Inn**	*01823 327513*
		East Reach, Taunton, TA1 3HT		
45	F4	**Near Tetbury**	**Holford Arms**	*01454 238669*
		Knockdown, Nr Tetbury, GL8 8QY		
29	F2	**Torquay**	**London Inn**	*01803 380003*
		The Strand, Torquay, TQ1 2AA		
29	F2	**Torquay**	**The Famous Hop'N'Grapes**	*01803 296814*
		Lower Union Lane, Torquay, TQ2 5PR		
29	F2	**Torquay**	**The Jolly Judge**	*01803 213848*
		Union Street, Torquay, TQ2 5QP		
29	F2	**Torquay**	**The Palms Hotel**	*0180 3293970*
		Babbacombe Road, Torquay, TQ1 1HQ		www.palmshoteltorquay.co.uk
29	F2	**Torquay**	**The Pickwick Inn**	*01803 298613*
		1 Pimlico, Torquay, TQ1 1EU		
35	D5	**Weymouth**	**Finn M'Couls**	*01305 778098*
		Westham Road, Weymouth, DT4 8NU		
35	D5	**Weymouth**	**The Black Dog**	*01305 771426*
		St Mary Street, Weymouth, DT4 8PB		
35	D5	**Weymouth**	**The Dolphin**	*01305 786751*
		Park Street, Weymouth, DT4 7DE		
35	D5	**Weymouth**	**The Dorothy Inn**	*01305 766996*
		The Esplanade, Weymouth, DT4 8DQ		
35	D5	**Weymouth**	**The Ferrybridge Inn**	*01305 760689*
		Portland Road, Wyke Regis, Weymouth, DT4 9AF		
34	C1	**Yeovil**	**Globetrotters**	*01935 423328*
		South Street, Yeovil, BA20 1QF		www.theglobetrotters.co.uk
34	C1	**Yeovil**	**Harry's Bar**	*01935 432143*
		Salisbury Road, Yeovil, BA20 1NR		
34	C1	**Yeovil**	**Porter Blacks**	*01935 429753*
		66 Middle Street, Yeovil, BA20 1LX		
34	C1	**Yeovil**	**The Butchers Arms**	*01935 428932*
		13 Hendford, Yeovil, BA20 1TQ		
34	C1	**Yeovil**	**The Plucknett**	*01935 476566*
		Peston Road, Yeovil, BA20 2EE		

Page/Ref	Town	Name	Telephone no.
	Address		Café website
44 C5	**Avonmouth**	**Avon Lodge**	*01179 827706*
	Third Way, Avonmouth, BS11 9YP		
36 B3	**Bournemouth**	**Als Diner**	*01202 399884*
	Holdenhurst Road, Bournemouth, BH8 8DA		
36 A3	**Bournemouth**	**Appetites Sandwich Bar**	*01202 296070*
	Yelverton Road, City Centre, Bournemouth, BH1 1DA		
36 B3	**Bournemouth**	**Bistro On The Beach**	*01202 431473*
	Solent Promenade, Southborne Coast Road, Bournemouth, BH6 4BE		www.bistroonthebeach.co.uk
36 A3	**Bournemouth**	**Café European**	*01202 296777*
	Exeter Road, Bournemouth, BH2 5AN		
36 A3	**Bournemouth**	**La Strada**	*01202 558902*
	Exeter Road, City Centre, Bournemouth, BH2 5AQ		www.italianlastrada.co.uk
36 A3	**Bournemouth**	**Yummies**	*01202 290322*
	Old Christchurch Road, City Centre, Bournemouth, BH1 1NU		
40 D4	**Bridgwater**	**Albion Inn & Truckstop**	*01458 210281*
	Bath Road, Ashcott, Bridgwater, TA7 9QT		
30 D3	**Bude**	**Atlantic Diner**	*01288 354167*
	Belle Vue, Bude, EX23 8JL		
30 D3	**Bude**	**Scrummies Café**	*01288 359522*
	Lansdown Road, Bude, EX23 8BH		
32 C5	**Chindleigh**	**Ibis Roadhouse Diner**	*01626 854033*
	Harcombe, Chindleigh, TQ13 0DF		
45 G5	**Chippenham**	**Silvey's**	*01249 750645*
	Draycot Cerne, Chippenham, SN15 5LH		
46 A2	**Cirencester**	**Greasy Joe's Café**	*01285 640275*
	Old Swindon Road, Cirencester, GL7 1NP		
33 E2	**Cullompton**	**The Willand Restaurant**	*01884 33603*
	Willand Service Station, Willand, Cullompton, EX15 2PF		
32 D4	**Exeter**	**Drakes Coffee House**	*01392 494470*
	Catherine Street, Exeter, EX1 1EX		
32 D4	**Exeter**	**Lord Sandwich**	*01392 421665*
	High Street, Exeter, EX4 3NZ		
32 D5	**Exeter**	**The Haldon Grill Café**	*01392 833700*
	A380, Telegraph Hill, Kennford, Exeter, EX6 7XW		
32 D4	**Exeter**	**The Milkmaid Restaurant**	*01392 277438*
	Catherine Street, Exeter, EX1 1EU		
41 G3	**Near Frome**	**Nunney Catch Café**	*01373 836331*
	Nunney Roundabout, Near Frome, BA11 4NZ		
45 F1	**Gloucester**	**Cardwarnines**	*01452 380028*
	Merchants Quay Unit 3, The Docks, Gloucester, GL1 2ER		
45 F1	**Gloucester**	**Lilys Sandwich Bar**	*01452 423680*
	Brunswick Road, Gloucester, GL1 1HG		
45 F1	**Gloucester**	**Sweet Success Tearooms**	*01452 383893*
	St Johns Lane, Gloucester, GL1 2AT		
45 F1	**Gloucester**	**Taipan Chinese Takeaway**	*01452 722838*
	13 School Lane, Quedgeley, Gloucester, GL2 4PP		
45 F1	**Gloucester**	**The Bus Station Café**	*01452 528104*
	Bruton Way, Gloucester, GL1 1DG		
45 F1	**Gloucester**	**The Oliver Twist**	*01452 381773*
	Northgate Street, Gloucester, GL1 1SL		
45 F1	**Gloucester**	**Zac's Deli**	*01452 521212*
	80 Eastgate Street, Gloucester, GL1 1QN		
24 C3	**Hayle**	**Café 1**	*01736 756123*
	Rose-an-grouse, Hayle, TR27 6LP		
33 G3	**Honiton**	**Newcott Chef**	*01404 861277*
	A303 Yarcombe, Honiton, EX14 9ND		

Page/Ref		Town Address	Name	Telephone no. Café website
28	B3	**Ivybridge**	**The Westwood Café**	*01752 894344*
		Old A38, Lee Mill, Ivybridge, PL21 9EF		
30	D5	**Launceston**	**Pie Stop Ltd**	*01566 782014*
		A30 Plusha Altarnum, Launceston, PL15 7RR		
40	C4	**North Petherton**	**Graham's Café**	*01278 663052*
		Taunton Road, North Petherton, TA6 6PR		
32	A4	**Okehampton**	**The Whitehouse Restaurant**	*01837 840101*
		A30 Exeter Road, Tongue End, Okehampton, EX20 1QJ		
24	B3	**Penzance**	**Dockers Rest Café**	*01736 362405*
		Wharf Road, Penzance, TR18 4AA		
24	B3	**Penzance**	**Mackerel Sky Café**	*01736 366866*
		New Street, Penzance, TR18 2LZ		
24	B3	**Penzance**	**The Bay**	*01736 363117* www.bay-penzance.co.uk
		Britons Hill, Penzance, TR18 3AE		
28	A3	**Plymouth**	**D&M's Café**	*01752 227933*
		Frankfort Gate, Plymouth, PL1 1QD		
28	A3	**Plymouth**	**Jakes**	*01752 222523*
		Cornwall Street, Plymouth, PL1 1NX		
28	A3	**Plymouth**	**Samantha's Takeaway**	*01752 665046*
		119 Cornwall Street, Plymouth, PL1 1PA		
36	B2	**Ringwood**	**Avon Heath Café**	*01425 471641*
		Brocks Pine, St Leonards, Ringwood, BH24 2DH		
43	E4	**Salisbury**	**Hilltop**	*01980 863086* www.thehilltop.co.uk
		A30, London Road, Firsdown, Salisbury, SP5 1ST		

Bikers welcome! We are open 7 days a week 8am-6pm (8pm on Friday) with ample parking. Fully licensed 84 seater with an extensive selection of all-day breakfasts, filled baps, jacket potatoes & baguettes. Chargrill special, steaks, gammons, BBQ Chicken and Chef's specials all cooked from fresh.

Page/Ref		Town Address	Name	Telephone no. Café website
42	D4	**Salisbury**	**Kelly's**	*01722 412431*
		Fisherton Street, Salisbury, SP2 7RB		
27	G3	**Saltash**	**Windy Ridge Eating House**	*01752 851036*
		A38 Trerulefoot, Saltash, PL12 5BJ		
33	G1	**Taunton**	**Biddy's Burger Bar**	*01823 257222*
		Station Road, Taunton, TA1 1NH		
33	G1	**Taunton**	**Brazz**	*01823 252000* www.brazz.co.uk
		Castle Bow, Taunton, TA1 1NF		
33	G1	**Taunton**	**Bumbles**	*01823 270705*
		Magdalene Lane, Taunton, TA1 1SE		
33	G1	**Taunton**	**Mr Cs Coffee Brasserie**	*01823 334191*
		County Walk, Taunton, TA1 3TZ		
33	G1	**Taunton**	**Studio Café**	*01823 271034*
		Bath Place, Taunton, TA1 4EP		
29	E2	**Torquay**	**RJ's Café**	*01386 881521*
		The Aller Layby, Torquay Road, Kingskerwell, Torquay, TQ12 5AT		
35	G3	**Wimborne**	**Vines Close Farm**	*01258 857278*
		Dorchester Road, Henbury, Wimborne, BH21 3RW		
34	C1	**Yeovil**	**Alpacinos**	*01935 433668*
		High Street, Yeovil, BA20 1RG		
34	C1	**Yeovil**	**Josie's Café**	*01935 433581*
		Pen Mill Trading Estate 1, Oxford Road, Yeovil, BA21 5HR		
34	C1	**Yeovil**	**The Gorge Café**	*01935 422370*
		Glovers Walk, Yeovil, BA20 1LH		
41	D5	**Near Yeovil**	**Jolly Diner**	*01935 822636*
		Tintinhull, Near Yeovil, BA22 8PF		

Page/Ref		Town / Address	Name	Telephone no. / Restaurant website
28	D1	**Ashburton**	**Holne Chase**	*01364 631471*
		Tavistock Road, Near Ashburton, TQ13 7NS		www.holne-chase.co.uk
29	D2	**Near Ashburton**	**The Rising Sun Inn**	*01364 652544*
		Woodland, Near Ashburton, TQ13 7JT		www.risingsunwoodland.co.uk
41	G1	**Bath**	**Moghul Indian Restaurant**	*01225 464956*
		Walcot Street, Bath, BA1 5BL		
41	F1	**Bath**	**The Hunts Rest Inn**	*01761 452303*
		Clifton Hill, Bath, BS39 5QL		www.huntsrest.co.uk
35	F3	**Bere Regis**	**The Royal Oak**	*01929 471203*
		West Street, Bere Regis, BH20 7HQ		www.theroyaloakhotel.co.uk
35	G2	**Blandford**	**The Anvil Inn**	*01258 453431*
		Salisbury Road, Pimperne, Blandford, DT11 8UQ		www.anvilinn.co.uk
36	A3	**Bournemouth**	**Bournemouth Tandoori**	*01202 296204*
		Holdenhurst Road, Bournemouth, BH8 8AD		
36	A3	**Bournemouth**	**Chez Fred**	*01202 761023*
		Seamoor Road, Westbourne, Bournemouth, BH4 9AN		www.chezfred.co.uk
36	A3	**Bournemouth**	**Ciao Restaurant**	*01202 555657*
		Old Christchurch Road, Town Centre, Bournemouth, BH1 1NL		www.ciaobournemouth.co.uk
36	A3	**Bournemouth**	**Lee's Dynasty**	*01202 532050*
		Wimborne Road, Winton, Bournemouth, BH9 2EY		
36	A3	**Bournemouth**	**Romanzo Greek Taverna**	*01202 761070*
		87 Poole Road, Westbourne, Bournemouth, BH4 9BB		
36	A3	**Bournemouth**	**The Chippy**	*01202 557669*
		90 Old Christchurch Road, Bournemouth, BH1 1LR		
28	D2	**Buckfastleigh**	**The Abbey Inn**	*01364 642343*
		Buckfast Road, Buckfast, Buckfastleigh, TQ11 0EA		www.abbey-inn.co.uk
30	D3	**Bude**	**The Widemouth Manor Hotel**	*01288 361263*
		Widemouth Bay, Bude, EX23 0DE		www.widemouthmanor.co.uk
46	A3	**Cirencester**	**The Wild Duck**	*01285 770310*
		Ewen, Cirencester, GL7 6BY		www.thewildduckinn.co.uk
42	C2	**Devizes**	**The Millstream Bar and Restaurant**	*01380 848308*
		Marteen, Devizes, SN10 3RH		
35	E2	**Dorchester**	**Poachers Inn**	*01300 348358*
		Piddletrenthide, Dorchester, DT2 7QX		www.thepoachersinn.co.uk
39	F4	**Near Dunster**	**The Royal Oak Inn**	*01984 640319*
		Luxborough, Near Dunster, TA23 0SH		www.theroyaloakinnluxborough.co.uk
32	D4	**Exeter**	**@ Angela's**	*01392 499038*
		New Bridge Street, Exeter, EX4 3AH		www.sun-dogs.co.uk
32	D4	**Exeter**	**Blue Dragon Oriental Buffet**	*01392 272 881*
		Fore Street, Exeter, EX4 3AT		www.bluefishbrasserie.com
32	D4	**Exeter**	**Blue Fish Brasserie & Vue Bar**	*01392 493581*
		Queen Street, Exeter, EX4 3SR		
33	D5	**Exeter**	**Galley Fish Restaurant & Cabins**	*01392 876078*
		Fore Street, Topsham, Exeter, EX3 0HU		www.galleyrestaurant.co.uk
32	D4	**Exeter**	**Ganges Restaurant**	*01392 272630*
		Fore Street, Exeter, EX4 3AT		
32	D4	**Exeter**	**Old Timers Wine Bar & Restaurant**	*01392 477704*
		Little Castle Street, Exeter, EX4 3PX		
32	D4	**Exeter**	**The Thai Orchard**	*01392 214215*
		Cathedral Yard, Exeter, EX1 1HJ		
25	F3	**Falmouth**	**Rathgowry Hotel**	*01326 313482*
		Gyllyngvase Hill, Gyllyngvase Beach, Falmouth, TR11 4DN		www.rathgowry.co.uk
45	F1	**Gloucester**	**Jewel in the Crown**	*01452 310366*
		Westgate Street, Gloucester, GL1 2NZ		
45	F1	**Gloucester**	**Nicki's Taverna**	*01452 301359*
		Westgate Street, Gloucester, GL1 2PG		
45	F1	**Gloucester**	**Taste of Thai**	*01452 520894*
		Southgate Street, Gloucester, GL1 1UT		

Page/Ref	Town Address	Name	Telephone no. Restaurant website
45 F1	**Gloucester** 8 Hare Lane, Gloucester, GL1 5LJ	Ye Olde Restaurant & Fish Shoppe	01452 522502
41 E5	**Ilchester** Ilchester, BA22 8LD	Northover Manor Hotel	01935 840447 www.northovermanor.com
24 A4	**Near Lands End** Sennen Cove, Near Lands End, TR19 7DG	The Old Success Inn	01736 871232 www.oldsuccess.com
38 D3	**Lynmouth** Harbourside, Lynmouth, EX35 6EG	The Rising Sun Hotel	01598 753223 www.specialplace.co.uk
46 C5	**Marlborough** Marlborough Road, Ogbourne St George, Marlborough, SN8 1SQ	The Inn With The Well	01672 841445 www.theinnwiththewell.co.uk
42 A4	**Mere** The Square, Mere, BA12 6DR	The George Inn	01747 860427 www.pubsulike.co.uk
45 F3	**Nailsworth** Nailsworth, GL6 0AE	Egypt Mill Hotel	01453 833449 www.egyptmill.com
31 G4	**Okehampton** Sourton Down, Okehampton, EX20 4HT	Prewley Moor	01837 861349
29 E3	**Paignton** Alta Vista Road, Roundham, Paignton, TQ4 6DB	Benbows Hotel	01803 558128
29 E2	**Paignton** Colin Road, Paignton, TQ3 2NR	Innisfree Hotel	01803 550692 www.innisfreehotel.co.uk
24 B3	**Penzance** 3 Albert Street, Penzance, TR18 2LR	Balti Spice	01736 364477
24 B4	**Penzance** The Strand, Newlyn, Penzance, TR18 5HW	China Garden	01736 367483
24 B3	**Penzance** New Street, Penzance, TR18 2LZ	Harris's Restaurant	01736 364408 www.harrissrestaurant.co.uk
24 A3	**Penzance** The Square, Pendeen, Penzance, TR19 7DN	The North Inn	01736 788417 www.thenorthinnpendeen.co.uk
24 A3	**Penzance** Market Square, St Just, Penzance, TR19 7HD	Wellington Hotel	01736 787319 www.wellington-hotel.co.uk
28 A3	**Plymouth** Mutley Plain, Plymouth, PL4 6JQ	Amora Pizza Bar	01752 257139
28 B3	**Plymouth** Radford Park Road, Plymouth, PL9 9DG	Baba's Indian Takeaway	01752 484441
28 A3	**Plymouth** Southside Street, Plymouth, PL1 2LE	Barbican Fish Bar	01752 261432
28 A3	**Plymouth** Embankment Road, Plymouth, PL4 9HY	China Express	01752 227633
28 A3	**Plymouth** Prysten House, Finewell Street, Plymouth, PL1 2AE	Tanners Restaurant	01752 252001 www.tannersrestaurant.com
28 A3	**Plymouth** Old Town Street, Plymouth, PL1 1DA	Warrens Bakery	01752 663862
25 E1	**St. Agnes** Trevaunance Cove, St. Agnes, TR5 0RT	Driftwood Spars Hotel	01872 552428 www.driftwoodspars.com
42 D5	**Salisbury** New Street, Salisbury, SP1 2PH	Apres LXIX	01722 340000
42 D4	**Salisbury** 60-64 Fisherton Street, Salisbury, SP2 7RB	Cheung's Chinese Restaurant	01722 321375
42 D5	**Salisbury** Ox Row, Salisbury, SP1 1EU	Harper's Restaurant	01722 333118
42 D5	**Salisbury** Milford Street, Salisbury, SP1 2AP	La Luna	01722 502191
42 D4	**Salisbury** South Western Road, Salisbury, SP2 7RR	Marrakech	01722 411112 www.lemarrakech.co.uk
42 D4	**Salisbury** 140 Fisherton Street, Salisbury, SP2 7QT	Rajpoot Tandoori Restaurant	01722 334795
43 D5	**Near Salisbury** The Ridge, Woodfalls, Near Salisbury, SP5 2LN	The Woodfalls Inn	01725 513222 www.woodfallsinn.co.uk

Page/Ref	Town Address	Name	Telephone no. Restaurant website
41 F4	**Near Shepton Mallet** Ditchet, Near Shepton Mallet, BA4 6RB	The Manor House Inn	01749 860276 www.manorhouseinn.co.uk
46 B4	**Swindon** Faringdon Road, Swindon, SN1 5AR	Aby's Indian	01793 514115 www.abysindian.co.uk
46 A4	**Swindon** Hook, Near Wootton Bassett, Swindon, SN4 8DZ	Bolingbroke Arms	01793 852357 www.thebolingbroke.co.uk
46 B4	**Swindon** Godwin Court, Old Town, Swindon, SN1 4BB	Jade Garden	01793 611199 www.swindonweb.com/jadegarden
46 B3	**Swindon** The Avenue, Stanton Fitzwarren, Swindon, SN6 7SD	Mt Fuji Restaurant	08700 841388 www.stantonhouse.co.uk
46 B4	**Swindon** Pepperbox Hill, Peatmoor, Swindon, SN5 5YZ	Pagoda Palace	01793 877888 www.pagodapalace.co.uk
46 B4	**Swindon** Commercial Road, Swindon, SN1 5PL	Parasol	01793 533188 www.parasol-oriental.com
33 G1	**Taunton** Station Road, Taunton, TA1 1PB	Dynasty Indian Cuisine	01823 334961
33 G1	**Taunton** 6 Shuttern, Taunton, TA1 4ET	Franco's Restaurant	01823 272480
33 G1	**Taunton** Upper Holway Road, Taunton, TA1 2QA	Holway Fish & Chip Shop	01823 322272
33 G1	**Taunton** Eastleigh Road, Taunton, TA1 2YE	Sea Horse Fish Bar	01823 353833
33 G1	**Taunton** Heron Gate, Taunton, TA1 2LP	Tramontes	0800 3292101
33 G1	**Taunton** Tower Lane, off Tower Street, Taunton, TA1 4AR	Willow Tree	01823 352835
30 B5	**Tintagel** Alantic Road, Tintagel, PL34 0DD	Wootons Country Hotel	01840 770170
29 F2	**Torquay** Torwood Street, Torquay, TQ1 1DT	Al Beb	01803 211755 www.albeb.co.uk
29 F2	**Torquay** Abbey Road, Torquay, TQ2 5NF	Balti Garden	01803 290087 www.baltigardenrestaurant.co.uk
29 F2	**Torquay** Torwood Street, Torquay, TQ1 1EB	Biancos Ristorante Italiano	01803 293430 www.biancos.co.uk
29 F2	**Torquay** Babbacombe Road, Babbacombe, Torquay, TQ1 3SW	Hanbury's Fish & Chips	01803 314616
29 F2	**Torquay** Beacon Terrace, Torquay, TQ1 2BH	No. 7 Fish Bistro	01803 295055 www.no7-fish.com
29 F2	**Torquay** 172 Union Street, Torquay, TQ2 5QP	The Vanilla Pod	01803 294414 www.thevanillapod.com
42 B3	**Warminster** Corton, Warminster, BA12 0SZ	The Dove Inn	01985 850109 www.thedove.co.uk
35 D5	**Weymouth** 24 Commercial Road, Weymouth, DT4 7DW	Balti House Tandoori Restaurant	01305 766347
35 D5	**Weymouth** Hope Square, Weymouth, DT4 8TR	Galley Bistro	01305 784059
35 D5	**Weymouth** St Thomas Street, Weymouth, DT4 4AW	Marlboro Restaurant	01305 785700
35 D5	**Weymouth** Trinity Road, The Old Harbour, Weymouth, DT4 8TJ	Perry's Restaurant	01305 785799
35 D5	**Weymouth** Hope Square, Weymouth, DT4 8TR	The Crows Nest Restaurant	01305 786930 www.crowsnestweymouth.co.uk
35 D4	**Weymouth** Littlemoor Road, Weymouth, DT3 6AF	The Golden Flame	01305 834018
34 C1	**Yeovil** North Terrace, Grass Royal, Yeovil, BA21 4JP	Grass Royal Fish & Chips Bar	01935 423084
34 C1	**Yeovil** Bunford Lane, Yeovil, BA20 2EJ	Palmers Fish & Chips	01935 434258

Page/Ref		Club name	Date of meet
		Meet venue & address	Website
45	G5	**A4 Riders Motorcycle Society**	*Monday nights*
		Lysley Arms, Pewsham, Chippenham, SN15 3RU	www.the-arms.co.uk
41	E4	**Allzorts Bikers Club**	*2nd Wednesday*
		Cross Keys, Lydford-on-Fosse, Somerton, TA11 7HA	www.allzorts-bikers.co.uk
38	B4	**Barnstaple and District MCC**	*1st Wednesday*
		The Rolle Quay, Rolle Quay, Barnstaple, EX31 1JE	www.bdmcc.co.uk
41	G1	**Bath University Motorcycle Club**	*Thursday nights*
		Plug, Bath University, Claverton Down, Bath, BA2 3AY	www.people.bath.ac.uk/su6cycle
31	F2	**Bikers Association of North Devon**	*Thursday nights*
		The Old Union Inn, Stibb Cross, Torrington, EX38 8LH	www.bikersassociationofnorthdevon.co.uk
27	E1	**Bolventor BMF**	*1st Sunday*
		Jamaica Inn, Bolventor, Launceston, PL15 7TS	
44	C5	**Bristol & Avon Roadrunners Motorcycle Club**	*3rd Wednesday*
		The Colosseum Pub, Redcliff Hill, Bristol, BS1 6SJ	www.bristolandavonroadrunners.co.uk
41	F1	**Bristol & Bath BMF**	*Last Monday*
		The Ship, 93 Temple St, Keynsham, Bristol, BS31 1ER	
46	A4	**Domine De Mortis MCC**	*Wednesdays*
		Beaufort Arms, Station Road, Wootton Bassett, Swindon, SN4 7EQ	
36	A3	**Dorset Motorcycle Association**	*1st & 3rd Monday*
		Albion Pub, 470 Ringwood Road, Poole, BH12 3LY	
35	G4	**Dorset Motorcycle Enthusiasts Club**	*3rd Monday*
		Sandford Inn, Sandford, North Wareham, BH20 7AD	www.dmec.cjb.net
44	A5	**Junction 20 Motorcycle Club**	*3rd Thursday*
		Salthouse Inn, Salthouse Road, Clevedon, BS21 7TY	www.junction20.fsnet.co.uk
24	C3	**Motorcycle Action Group**	*1st Thursday*
		The Royal Standard Inn, 50 Churchtown Avenue, Gwinear, TR27 5JL	www.south-west-region.mag-uk.org
40	C3	**National Association for Bikers with a Disability**	*3rd Tuesday*
		Watchfield Inn, Watchfield, Near Burnham On Sea, TA9 4RD	www.nabd.org.uk
44	D5	**New Sentinels M.R.C.**	*Thursdays*
		Rhubarb Tavern, 30 Queen Ann Road, Barton Hill, Bristol, BS5 9TX	www.new-sentinels.co.uk
30	B5	**North Cornwall MCC**	*last Tuesday*
		King Arthur's Arms Pub, Fore Street Tintagel, PL34 0DA	www.ncmcc.co.uk
31	F1	**North Devon British Motorcycle Owners Club**	*2nd & 4th Thursday*
		Pollyfield Centre, Bideford, EX39 4BL	www.ndbmoc.freeserve.co.uk
45	G3	**Ogri MCC**	*See website*
		Kemble Airfield, Kemble, near Cirencester, GL7 6BA	www.ogrimcc.org
29	E2	**Paighton bike nights**	*Every Wednesday*
		Paighton seafront, Paighton	www.holidaytorbay.co.uk/htbikenights.html
43	E1	**Pewsey BMF**	*2nd Wednesday*
		The Bruces Arms Pub, Eastern Royal Road, Eastern Royal, Pewsey, SN9 5LR	
28	A3	**Plymouth Advanced Motorcyclists Group**	*2nd Monday*
		Parkway Sports & Social Club, Ernesettle Lane, Plymouth, PL5 2EY	www.plymouthadvancedmotorcyclists.org.uk
28	A3	**Plymouth MMC**	*Every other Monday*
		Plymouth City Bus Social Club, Alma Road, Milehouse, Plymouth, PL3 4AA	www.plymouthmcc.org.uk
36	A3	**Poole Quay Dream Machines**	*Every Tuesday*
		Poole Quay, Poole	www.pooletourism.com
43	D5	**Salisbury MAG**	*Monday nights*
		The Stag Inn, Charlton All Saints, SP5 4HD	
29	E1	**South Devon BMF**	*1st Tuesday*
		The Ten Tors Pub, Exeter Road, Kingsteignton, Newton Abbot, TQ12 3NP	
42	B5	**South West Bike'n'Trike Social Club**	*1st Tuesday*
		The South Western Public House, Station Road, Tisbury, SP3 6JR	
28	A3	**The BLUE KNIGHTS© Law Enforcement Motorcycle Club**	*2nd Saturday*
		The Hideaway Cafe, Units 24 & 25 Faraday, Mill, Prince Rock, Plymouth, PL4 0ST	www.bkengland14.org.uk
42	B1	**West Wilts Motor Club Ltd**	*1st Thursday*
		Melksham House, Melksham, SN12 6ES	www.wwmc.co.uk
45	G5	**Wild Roses Lady Riders**	*Tuesday nights*
		King Alfred Inn, Malmesbury Rd, Chippenham, SN15 1QA	www.wildrosesladyriders.co.uk
42	A1	**Wiltshire TRF**	*1st Tuesday*
		Bell on the Common, The Common, Broughton, SN12 8LX	www.wiltshiretrf.co.uk

Torbay Motorcycles

We are a friendly local dealership with over 40 years experience as Honda main dealer, we aim to cater for all customers providing the care and attention that has kept us in business all these years and keeps our customers coming back for more.

We offer new and used bike sales with the backup you would expect from a Honda main dealer along side parts, clothing, accessories and full workshop facilities.

Despite our town centre location we have off road motorcycle parking at the rear of our shop.

87 Queen Street
Newton Abbot
Devon TQ12 2BG
01626 352527
www.torbaymc.eclipse.co.uk

www.thepieguide.com

To advertise here, or in any of our **Regional Bike Guides** Please contact: tony@thepieguide.com Tel: (020) 7324 6126

The South West Bike Guide
Part of the Open Road Rider's Guide Series

London Bike Guide
Third edition

Muc-Off

bike cleaning made easy

[8 IN 1 PIT KIT]

VISIT OUR WEBSITE TO
BUY ONLINE
OR FIND A DEALER

BEFORE   AFTER!

www.muc-off.com

THE RIDER'S DIGEST

www.theridersdigest.co.uk

The **FREE** magazine that's grabbing rider's attention from Dover to Bristol, and Portsmouth to Northampton.

Check our website to locate your copy of the best motorcycle writing on the streets – probably, and details of our ludicrously cheap subscription offer.

www.theridersdigest.co.uk

MOTORCYCLE & SCOOTER CENTRE

Main dealers for:
Kawasaki – Aprilia – Piaggio – Gilera –
Vespa   Derbi & Victory

Over 100 New and Used machines in stock

Torbay's Premier dealers for all your motorcycling needs.

Sales – Repairs – MOT's - Training – Clothing &
Accessories – Finance – Insurance – Part Exchange
& other specialist services.

Why not pay us a visit at:

Broomhill Way Torquay TQ2 7QL
Phone 01803 616164
Web: www.pghmotorcycles.com

WINNER
2006 DEALER
OF THE YEAR

Best New Outlet

SUPERBIKE CENTRE
www.speedthrills.co.uk

One of the biggest selections of used muscle,
custom and superbikes in the South West.

Tel 01392 211246
Mob 07968 020224

King Edward Street, Cowley Bridge Road, Exeter EX4 4NY

'Clothing chosen for women by women'

GIRLSbike2
'Clothing chosen for women by women'

CLOTHING CHOSEN
FOR WOMEN BY WOMEN

The only retailer selling motorbike clothes and accessories
just for women, offering an unrivalled choice
of brands, size, colour and style in a 'boutique' style
environment with excellent customer service and advice...

• Unique boutique style stores just for women
• The widest range of motorbike clothing designed
  for women under one roof
• Relaxed female orientated shopping experience
• Sizes 6 – 26
• Range of styles, designs, colours and fit
• Knowledgeable and experienced female staff
• Exclusive GirlsBike2 ranges and styles
• Excellent customer service
• Coffee available while you browse

GirlsBike2 Poole
166 - 168 Ashley Road,
Poole, Dorset,
BH14 9BY
T 01202 717427
www.girlsbike2.com

'Clothing chosen for women by women'

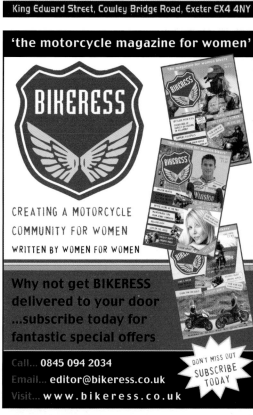

'the motorcycle magazine for women'

BIKERESS

CREATING A MOTORCYCLE
COMMUNITY FOR WOMEN
WRITTEN BY WOMEN FOR WOMEN

Why not get BIKERESS
delivered to your door
...subscribe today for
fantastic special offers

Call... 0845 094 2034
Email... editor@bikeress.co.uk
Visit... www.bikeress.co.uk

DON'T MISS OUT
SUBSCRIBE
TODAY

Next in the Series:

There are 10 guides in the series. Currently available are the London and South West Regions. The remaining regions available later this year include: Scotland, North East, Midlands, East, South, North West, Wales and Northern Ireland. To reserve an advance copy please email: **lucy@thePIE guide.com** and state which region/s you want.

Feedback

If you have any general comments either about the guide or about regional rider's guides we would like to hear from you. If there are specific areas not covered by this guide which you would like to see added, please comment directly by email: **swguide@thepieguide.com**

About Us

PIE (Public Information Exchange) produces customised map-based products for different driving sectors including motorbike and scooter riders, disabled (Blue Badge) drivers, van, coach & lorry drivers.

We also supply bespoke online mapping and content overlay solutions as well as selling the raw content to clients for use with their own applications.

New recommendations

If during your travels you feel that a site, be it accommodation, bar, restaurant or café, needs to be on our map please let us know. You can either download a recommendation form from the **www.parkingforbikes.com** site or text your recommendations to 07949 68 339.

Products include the interactive and functional site mapping application: **www.completedirections.com**

 completedirections

Our contact details:
PIE Enterprises Ltd
The Bridge 12-16 Clerkenwell Road,
London, EC1M 5PQ
Tel: 0870 444 5434
Email: **info@thePIEguide.com**

Web site owners

If you have a website you can be an affiliate by promoting this and any other PIE products and make commissions on all sales made. To sign up email Lucy on: **lucy@thePIEguide.com**

Online solutions include:
www.parkingforbikes.com
www.parkingforvans.com
www.roadsforbikes.com
www.routesforbikes.com
www.londonlorrycontrol.com
www.parkingforbluebadges.com

Reseller & Distributors

To become a reseller or distributor of this or any other PIE guides contact Lucy at PIE on 0870 444 5434 or email: **lucy@thepieguide.com**